Teaching Information & Technology Skills: The Big6™ in Secondary Schools

By Michael B. Eisenberg and Robert E. Berkowitz
With Robert Darrow and Kathleen L. Spitzer

Linworth Publishing, Inc.
Worthington, Ohio

Library of Congress Cataloging-in-Publication Data

Eisenberg, Michael.
    Teaching information & technology skills : the Big6 in secondary schools / Michael B.
Eisenberg and Robert E. Berkowitz ; with Robert Darrow and Kathleen L. Spitzer.
       p. cm.
    Includes bibliographical references (p.) and index.
    ISBN 1-58683-006-6
    1. Information retrieval--Study and teaching (Secondary) 2. Information retrieval--Study
and teaching (Secondary)--United States. 3. Electronic information resource literacy--Stud
and teaching (Secondary) 4. Electronic information resource literacy--Study and teaching
(Secondary)--United States. I. Title: Teaching information and technology skills.
    II. Berkowitz, Robert E.

    ZA3075 .E425 2000
    025.04'071'2--dc21
00-060592
CIP

Published by Linworth Publishing, Inc.
480 East Wilson Bridge Road, Suite L
Worthington, Ohio 43085

ISBN 1-58683-006-6
5 4 3 2 1

Table of Contents

Table of Figures

List of Worksheets

Acknowledgements

First and foremost, we wish to thank Sue Wurster for making sure that this book was finished! As with the elementary book*, Sue was a tireless manager and editor who kept us on task and focused on quality. Without her help, we might still be writing and revising!

Second, we appreciate the high quality work of our partnering contributors, Rob Darrow and Kathy Spitzer. Their expertise and creativity as master teachers and Big6ers are essential elements of this work.

Third, working with Marlene Woo-Lun and the team at Linworth continues to be a pleasure. High quality, a can-do attitude, and a fun group—what more could authors ask for?

Fourth, as the use and popularity of the Big6 explodes in schools around the world, it is increasingly hard to single out individuals for acknowledgment. Therefore, we wish to formally thank all Big6ers. Your work with students makes a difference—every day!

And, as always, we thank our families, the Eisenbergs, Carol, Brian and Laura, and the Berkowitzs, Joyce, Adam and Marette. Thanks again for all your encouragement, support, and understanding.

Mike Eisenberg & Bob Berkowitz

Eisenberg, M. B., & Berkowitz, R. E. (1999). Teaching information & technology skills: The Big6™ in elementary schools. Worthington, OH: Linworth Publishing, Inc.

Dedication

To Jeffrey Katzer. Incomparable.

To Joel Morris. Teacher and friend; a Mensch.

About the Authors and Contributors

Michael B. Eisenberg is director of the Information School of the University of Washington (Seattle). For many years, he was a faculty member at the School of Information Studies at Syracuse University and co-founder of the Information Institute of Syracuse, (which includes AskERIC, the award winning online information service for the K–12 community). His work focuses on the use of information and information technology by individuals and organizations to meet their information needs and manage their information more effectively and efficiently. Mike conducts research, writes, consults, and lectures frequently on information problem-solving, information technology, the Internet, and information management in learning and teaching.

Mike is a graduate of State University of New York at Albany (B.A. and M.L.S). He earned a certificate of advanced studies and a Ph.D. in Information Transfer from Syracuse University.

Robert E. Berkowitz is high school library media specialist and K-12 advisor for library and information services at Wayne Central Schools (Ontario Center, NY). Bob has successfully managed school libraries for Head Start-12th grade in both rural and urban settings. He has been an educational professional since 1971. Bob is a strong believer in active, curriculum-centered library media programs and promotes the integration of information literacy skills across the entire curriculum. He consults with state education departments, school districts and local schools. He also shares his ideas at state, regional, and local conferences and seminars. Bob is an adjunct professor at Syracuse University's School of Information Studies and has taught at other institutions of higher education.

Bob is a graduate of the American International College, B.A. (Springfield, MA). He earned an M.A. in Education, George Washington University; M.L.S. State University of New York at Albany; and School Administrator's Certification, North Adams State College (North Adams, MA).

Rob Darrow is the library media teacher at Alta Sierra Intermediate School in Clovis, California. As a professional educator since 1975, he has taught every grade level from kindergarten to eighth grade. He promotes and uses the Big6 as a library media teacher in class lessons, throughout the school and district, and throughout the state of California. Rob develops Big6 lessons to teach students the use of technology and the World Wide Web. He hands out a Big6 bookmark to every student every year and tells them, "the better user of information you become, the better job you will get in the future. Using and applying the Big6 to everything you do will cause you to become an outstanding user of information, and ultimately, get you the best jobs!" He has presented workshops about the Big6 to parents, teachers, colleagues and students. He received the Outstanding Alumnus Award from Fresno Pacific University's Library Media Teacher Graduate Program in 1998. He studied under Mike Eisenberg and Bob Berkowitz as he earned his library media teacher credentials. Rob also serves as the webmaster for the California School Library Association (http://www.schoollibrary.org).

Rob is a graduate of the University of California, Riverside where he earned his B.A. in Political Science and his teaching credential. He subsequently earned his M.S. in Administrative Leadership and Supervision from San Jose State University and then his library media teacher credential from Fresno Pacific University.

Kathy Spitzer is a library media specialist at Cicero-North Syracuse High School (Cicero, New York). She serves on school level and district level technology, software and Web committees and maintains the library Web page.

As an active member of the North Syracuse Central Schools' Technology Cadre, Kathy develops and teaches courses on integrating various technologies into the curriculum. She presents workshops on topics ranging from promoting reading for secondary students to influencing the administration by actively reporting on the library media program. She has written numerous articles on integrating information skills and is the author of *Information Literacy: Essential Skills for the Information Age*, published in 1998. For the past three years, Kathy has served as an editor for the *Big6™ Newsletter* (now the *Big6™ eNewsletter*, http://www.big6.com/enewsletter).

Kathy is a member of ALA-AASL, NYLA, SLMS, NYSUT, Beta Phi Mu (National Library Honor Society), and Central New York Media Specialists. She was also a volunteer with KidsConnect and is a mentor for library media students enrolled in the School of Information Studies at Syracuse University.

Foreword

We are pleased to offer this companion book to our previous work focusing on the Big6 in elementary schools. As stated in the foreword to that book, "the Big6™ Skills approach to information & technology skills instruction is a systematic process that continually grows in sophistication as learners grow and develop." The Big6 is also growing in terms of application and use in schools.

We, therefore, offer this book to provide secondary school classroom teachers, teacher-librarians, and technology teachers with the background and tools necessary to implement an integrated Big6 program. The first part of this book explains the Big6 approach and the rationale behind it. Specific techniques, strategies, and ways to build the Big6 Skills into existing instructional programs will be also discussed, as well as ways to create new units and lessons.

This book includes specific sample Big6 instructional ideas in context which can be used as is or modified to meet specific instructional needs. These instructional ideas can provide the basis for developing a powerful information & technology skills instructional program.

Contributors to this volume are experienced educators. Together, we provide detailed information to help you get started or to expand your existing Big6 program.

Our philosophy is that in an information age, information & technology skills are basic education. We believe that library media specialists and other teachers need to encourage information based problem-solving and decision-making skills that empower students and improve literacy.

We hope that *Teaching the Big6™ in Secondary Schools* will be a major contribution to the field of information & technology skills instruction. Teachers using this book can change what happens in classrooms, library media centers, technology labs, and communities.

PART I
The BIG 6

Overview of the Big6™ Approach

CHAPTER 1

Introduction: The Need and the Solution

The Need—Living in an Information Society

It's almost a cliché to say that we live in an increasingly complex world, an information age. However, that doesn't make it any less true or any less difficult to manage. And, just as students at the secondary level are more sophisticated than those in elementary school, the nature and scope of their information problems are also more sophisticated and complicated. They too are overwhelmed by the information explosion and suffer from information anxiety.

Here are some statistics that describe the information explosion that all of us face every day:

- A weekday edition of the *New York Times* has more information in it than the average 17th century man or woman would have come across in an entire lifetime (Lewis, 1996).

- In this half-century, for the first time in history, the capacity for producing information is far greater than the human capacity to process it (Shenk, 1997).

- Regarding the estimated number of Web pages: in 1995: 1.3 million; in January 2000: more than 1 billion! (Guernsey, 2000).

Information anxiety is rampant. People even get physically sick as a result of the stress caused by information overload. It's true, and it's even got its own medical term: Information Fatigue Syndrome (*Investor's Business Daily*, 1996). A study reported in the *Texas Library Journal* (Akin, 1998) noted that some of the symptoms associated with information overload are:

- Fatigue
- Stomach pains
- Failing eyesight
- Insomnia
- Forgetfulness
- Feeling overwhelmed
- Stress
- Doubt
- Vulnerability
- Anxiousness
- Computer rage

There's simply too much information being created, stored, processed, and presented. Being overloaded is the norm; people just can't keep up. And we aren't just talking about people in the workforce or higher education. Even elementary students are having difficulties meeting the information demands.

Dr. Melissa Gross recently studied the information behaviors of school-age children. Dr. Gross (1998) looked at why students were searching for information, comparing self-driven questions and needs to questions and needs imposed by others—including teachers. Not surprisingly, she found that as students progress in school, they search less and less for their own purposes. Older students search for information almost exclusively in response to imposed needs. By the time students enter high school, they spend a great deal of time reacting to information demands placed upon them by others.

Gross' findings confirm our own observations concerning the reading habits of K-12 students. In the lower grades, students have more time to read for pleasure, and take more time to read on their own. But, as they get older, students have less time for their own reading or to pursue their own interests. The demands imposed on them—the information demands—are substantial in terms of what they are asked to do as well as the difficulties of finding, processing, and presenting information.

Again, there's just too much "stuff" out there, and it's not easy to keep up. At the same time, there's an irony—yes, we are surrounded by information, but we can never seem to find what we want, when we want it, and in the form we want it.

One solution to the information problem—the one that seems to be most often adopted in schools (as well as in business and society in general)—is to speed things up. We try to pack in more and more content, to work faster to get more done. But, this is a losing proposition. It's like that old *I Love Lucy* show (Ball, 1952)—the one with Lucy and Ethel on the candy factory line. The candy comes through on the conveyor belt, and Lucy and Ethel are to wrap each piece of candy. They start out fine, feeling pretty good and saying things like, "This is easy." "We can handle this." But soon the candy is moving faster and faster. They start struggling, pulling the candy off the belt, stuffing the pieces under their hats, in their mouths, and in their uniforms while exclaiming, "We're fighting a losing game!"

In education too, speeding things up can only work for so long. Instead, we need to think about helping students to work smarter, not faster. There is an alternative to speeding things up. It's the smarter solution, one that helps students develop the skills and understandings they need to find, process, and use information effectively. This smarter solution focuses on process as well as content. Some people call this smarter solution information literacy or information skills instruction. We call it the Big6.

The Big6™

The Big6 is a process model of how people of all ages solve an information problem. From practice and study, we found that successful information problem-solving encompasses six stages:

1. *Task Definition*
2. *Information Seeking Strategies*
3. *Location & Access*
4. *Use of Information*
5. *Synthesis*
6. *Evaluation*

People go through these Big6 stages—consciously or not—when they seek or apply information to solve a problem or make a decision. It's not necessary to complete these stages in a linear order, and a given stage doesn't need to take a lot of time. We have found that in almost all successful problem-solving situations, all stages are completed.

The Big6™ and Other Approaches

The Big6 shares some similarities with other process models. For example, one generic guide to improved problem-solving and creative thinking is Koberg and Bagnall's "Problem-Solving Feedback Perspective" from *The*

Universal Traveler (1980). Theirs is a seven-step approach that begins by accepting the existing situation or problem and moves to analyzing the components of the problem, defining the problem, brainstorming and selecting the solution, implementation, and evaluation. This model is characterized by its logical pattern that begins with understanding that a problem exists, and ends not with implementing a solution, but rather an evaluation of the effects of the action taken. This allows for reassessment to determine if the problem or any aspects of the problem still exist.

A process model widely used in gifted and talented education is the "Creative Problem Solving" model (Noller, Parnes, and Biondi, 1976). The five major steps in this model are:

- *Fact-finding:* Collect all data surrounding the problem.

- *Problem-finding:* Restate the problem in a more solvable form.

- *Idea-finding:* Brainstorm and defer judgment in an attempt to develop as many ideas as possible for solving the problem.

- *Solution-finding:* Select the criteria for evaluating solutions, and then apply the criteria to each possible solution. Choose the best solution.

- *Acceptance-finding:* Present the solution to all parties involved to decide if it would be workable. Plan, implement, and evaluate the solution.

There are also a number of information literacy process models coming from the library media field: Stripling and Pitts (1988), Kuhlthau (1985, 1993), Irving and others.

It is encouraging that there are more similarities among the models than differences (see chart below). That is, the driving force behind these models is "process." Information skills are not isolated incidents, but rather connected activities that encompass a way of thinking about and using information.

The Big6™ and K-12 National Information Literacy Standards

There are also major elements of the Big6 in recently developed national standards for K-12 and for higher education.

New K-12 information literacy standards were developed by the American Association of School Librarians and the Association of Educational Communications and Technology (1998) as part of the *Information Power: Building Partnerships for Learning* document. The first three of the standards emphasize abilities associated with information literacy. The information literate student:

- Accesses information efficiently and effectively (Standard 1).
- Evaluates information critically and competently (Standard 2).
- Uses information accurately and creatively (Standard 3).

(http://www.ala.org/aasl/ip_implementation.html)

COMPARISON CHART

Eisenberg/Berkowitz Information Seeking (The Big6 Skills)	Kuhlthau Information Problem-Solving	Irving Information Skills	Stripling/Pitts Research Process	New South Wales Information Process
1. Task Definition 1.1 Define the problem 1.2 Identify info requirements	1. Initiation 2. Selection 3. Formulation (of focus)	1. Formulation/analysis of information need	1. Choose a broad topic 2. Get an overview of the topic 3. Narrow the topic 4. Develop thesis/ purpose statement	Defining
2. Information Seeking Strategies 2.1 Determine range sources 2.2 Prioritize sources	4. Exploration (investig. info on the general topic) 5. Collection (gather info on the focused topic)	2. Identification/appraisal of like y sources 3. Tracing/locating individual resources 4. Examining, selecting, & rejecting indiv. resources	5. Formulate questions to guide research 6. Plan for research & production 7. Find, analyze, evaluate resources	Locating
3. Location & Access 3.1 Locate sources 3.2 Find info				Selecting
4. Information Use 4.1 Engage (read, view, etc.) 4.2 Extract info		5. Interrogating/using individual resources 6. Recording/storing info	8. Evaluate evidence take notes/compile bib.	Organizing
5. Synthesis 5.1 Organize 5.2 Present	6. Presentation	7. Interpretation, analysis, synthesis and eval. of info. 8. Shape, presentation, and communication of info	9. Formulate questions to guide research 10. Create and present final product	Presenting
6. Evaluation 6.1 Judge the product 6.2 Judge the process	7. Assessment (of outcome/process)	9. Evaluation of the assignment	(Reflection point—is the paper/project satisfactor	Assessing

Standard 1, accessing information, is similar to Big6 Skill #3–Location and Access, and Standard 3, uses information, relates to Big6 #4–Use of Information. Standard 2, evaluates information, permeates the Big6 process. That is, while it might be tempting to create a separate stage for evaluates information (coming between #4 Use of Information and #5 Synthesis, for example) we recognize that the information literate person evaluates information at every stage:

- *Stage #1 Task Definition*—evaluate the nature and type of information needed
- *Stage #2 Use of Information*—evaluate information among potential sources
- *Stage #3 Location & Access*—evaluate how to represent information as search terms
- *Stage #4 Use of Information*—evaluate what information is relevant and useful
- *Stage #5 Synthesis*—evaluate the specific information to apply to the task and how the information fits together
- *Stage #6 Evaluation*—evaluate the quality of information in the final product and effectiveness in the process.

The second set of three standards in *Information Power* relate to independent learning related to personal interests (Standard 4), appreciation of literature and other creative expressions of information (Standard 5), and striving for excellence in information seeking and knowledge generation (Standard 6).

The last set of three standards focus on social responsibility—contributing positively to the learning community. These standards include recognizing the importance of information to a democratic society (Standard 7), practicing ethical behavior in regard to information and information technology (Standard 8), and participating effectively in groups to pursue and generate information (Standard 9).

Higher Education

In 2000, the Association of College and Research Libraries published standards for information literacy in higher education. According to the introduction to the standards, this set of goals and outcomes was developed to encourage students to become lifelong learners (http://www.ala.org/acrl/ilintro.html). In other words, the standards describe a student who knows how to learn and has an agile mind that will adapt quickly to the changing information landscape.

The ACRL information literacy standards are as follows:

- *Standard One*—The information literate student determines the nature and extent of the information needed.
- *Standard Two*—The information literate student accesses needed

information effectively and efficiently.

- *Standard Three*—The information literate student evaluates information and its sources critically and incorporates selected information into his or her knowledge base and value system.

- *Standard Four*—The information literate student, individually or as a member of a group, uses information effectively to accomplish a specific purpose.

- *Standard Five*—The information literate student understands many of the economic, legal, and social issues surrounding the use of information and accesses and uses information ethically and legally.

(www.ala.org/acrl/ilstandardlo.html)

The ACRL standards focus on the student's information problem-solving process, rather than on discrete skills the student displays. Many of these standards relate to the Big6; for instance, Standard One is similar to Task Definition, in that not only is the student considering what needs to be done, but what kind of information is needed to do it. Standard Three is particularly interesting, since it incorporates the idea of the learner contextualizing knowledge—adding what they find into the framework of information they already know.

All of these approaches to teaching information literacy skills are valid and significant. The ACRL and *Information Power* standards broach significant issues for the information age, such as ethics and citizenship, while the Big6 focuses on the information problem-solving aspect of information literacy. Obviously, we prefer the Big6 to any other approach—we promote the Big6 because we have found it to be a teachable process that students can relate to, and above all, that works.

Despite its brevity compared to other processes, the Big6 is sufficient and necessary in that it encompasses the full range of the process—our research shows this. People who are natural problem solvers see themselves in the Big6 ("I've been doing this all along!"), and people who do not work as well with information find the Big6 to be a solution for many of their problems. The Big6 is widely applicable—not just for research reports and papers, but for real-life problems such as deciding on which college to attend or how to find a summer job. Finally, the Big6 is easy to remember—it is concise, expressive, and catchy. Once students learn it, it becomes a natural part of their information toolbox.

Learning and Teaching the Big6™

In addition to considering the Big6 as a process, another useful way to view the Big6 is as a set of basic, essential life skills. These skills can be applied across situations—to school, personal, and work settings. The Big6 Skills are applicable to all subject areas across the full range of grade levels. Students use the Big6 Skills whenever they need information to solve a problem, make a decision, or complete a task.

The Big6 Skills are best learned when integrated with classroom curriculum and activities. Teachers can begin to use the Big6 immediately by:

- Using the Big6 terminology when giving various tasks and assignments
- Talking students through the process for a particular assignment
- Asking key questions and focusing attention on specific Big6 actions to accomplish.

For example, suppose students are learning about World War II. They may start by answering a set of questions about the causes of the war or complete a worksheet or map. Later, students might take a test and also prepare a more extensive report or project. For each task that students are required to do, classroom teachers should ask, "What are you trying to accomplish? What types and how much information will you need to do it?" That's Big6 Stage #1, Task Definition.

From experience, we find that students have the most problems with Task Definition. At the same time, teachers, library media specialists, and even parents underestimate the difficulty of figuring out exactly what is to be done, the information needed to complete the task, what the result should look like once it's completed, and how the student is going to be assessed or graded.

Classroom teachers and library media specialists can use the Big6 to make an immediate impact on student performance by spending time on Task Definition whenever students get an assignment. That doesn't necessarily mean explaining the assignment and expectations in greater detail. Rather, it means developing techniques and lessons that help students learn to analyze an assignment, determine requirements, and get moving in the information problem-solving process.

After working on Task Definition, the teacher can then go through the rest of the Big6—prompting students to ensure that they consider the various aspects of the full process in relation to the assignment. Later, teachers or library media specialists can provide specific lessons on more Big6 stages— at the relevant time as the students work on their various assignments within the World War II unit. Chapter 4 provides more detail on implementation of the Big6, and the second part of this book includes examples in context.

Beyond incorporating the Big6 into everyday classroom practice, we recommend that teachers work with library media specialists and technology teachers to systematically plan to teach the Big6 Skills as part of the curriculum. Learning these essential information skills takes effort and repetition. Students need opportunities to develop in-depth expertise in each of the Big6 Skills. This requires a planned program of instruction and learning. Again, see Chapter 4 for more information on implementing the Big6.

Various computer and information technology skills are integral parts of the Big6 Skills. For example, when students use word processing to write a letter, that's Big6 #5, Synthesis. When they search for information on the World Wide Web, that's Big6 #3, Location & Access. When they use e-mail to discuss an assignment with another student or the teacher, that's Big6 #1, Task Definition. Using computers can "turbo-boost" students' abilities.

Teaching and learning to use technology as part of the Big6 process is very helpful for students and teachers. Students see the connection between various technology skills and how the skills can be applied to the completion of the project. Teachers have a context for integrating technology instruction into classroom learning, assignments, and projects. Instead of focusing on the technology itself, teachers can help students think about what they want to accomplish and think how technology might help them reach their goals. The Big6-technology connection is explored in Chapter 3. But first, it's time to focus on the Big6 itself, to dive into the Big6 process and skills in detail.

Summary

Developing general information problem-solving skills as well as proficiencies in specific technologies and information processes is a major focus in education today—K-12 as well as higher education The Big6 is a tried and tested approach to information and technology skills instruction. On the surface, the Big6 appears to be relatively simple and common sense. However, ensuring that students learn these fundamental skills for an information society takes concerted and planned effort in educational settings. Furthermore, we want our students to be more than simply aware or literate in terms of these skills; we want them to be fluent and able to demonstrate mastery across contexts.

The chapters that follow in Part I explain in more detail the Big6 model and skills; how technology is integral to Big6 use and vice versa; approaches to implementation of Big6 instruction; and finally how to assess Big6 learning. Part II provides a rich set of specific Big6 lessons and examples that can be easily adapted to a range of school and learning settings.

Reflections

CHAPTER 2

The Big6™ Process and Skills

A s explained in Chapter 1, the Big6 can be described both as a set of essential life skills and as a process. This is a strength of the Big6 approach—it provides a unified, process-context for learning and teaching information and technology skills.

We also find it's useful to explain the Big6 in a top-down fashion. That is, when working with students, we first try to have them understand that the Big6 is a process, from beginning to end. Then, we focus on the main six stages—from Task Definition to Evaluation. Finally, we have two sub-stages under each of the Big6. This results in twelve sub-stages, the "Little12." The various specific levels of the Big6 are presented in more detail below.

The Big6 is applicable to every age group and level of development—from Pre-K to senior citizen. For example, we present the idea of process and the Big6 to very young children with something called the "Super3." The three stages of the Super3 are:

- Beginning—Plan—What is my task?
- Middle—Do—What do I have to do to complete the task?
- End—Review—How will I know when I am done?

These three stages form an easy way to get young students to start thinking about how they will solve information problems. They learn about taking "steps" in a "process." Secondary school students, hopefully, will be skilled in these fundamental information problem-solving building blocks. Of course, for some students in certain situations (particularly those with learning problems), it may be desirable to start with the basics: plan—do—review.

However, as noted, the Big6 is also directly applicable in higher education and beyond. The information literacy standards identified as essential for success in higher education (developed by the Association of College and Research Libraries and endorsed by the American Association of Higher Education), closely resemble the Big6 Skills.

Levels of the Big6™

Level 1: The Conceptual Level

> *Whenever students are faced with an information-based problem to solve—e.g., homework, an assignment, test, quiz, or decision—they can use the Big6 approach.*

The broadest level of the Big6 approach is the conceptual or overview level. Here, we establish the concept of process and flow. Whether we realize it or not, we undertake a process with every assignment or information task. Recognizing the process and our personal preferences for problem-solving can help us be more effective and efficient. As part of this, at this broad level, we recommend helping students learn the following:

- Recognize that most problems have a strong information component; the problems are information-rich
- Recognize problems as such and to be able to identify the information aspects of that problem
- Realize that information-rich problems can be solved systematically and logically
- Understand that the Big6 Skills will help them solve the problem effectively and efficiently.

Level 2: The Big6™ *Skills*

The second level in the Big6 approach includes the set of six distinct skills that comprise the general problem-solving method: The Big6 Skills.

 1 Task Definition

 2 Information Seeking Strategies

 3 Location & Access

 4 Use of Information

 5 Synthesis

 6 Evaluation

When students are in a situation that requires information problem-solving, they should use these skills. We have found that completing each of these six stages successfully is necessary for solving information problems. The stages of the Big6 do not necessarily need to be completed in any particular order. Nor do students always need to be aware that they are engaging in a particular stage. However, at some point in time students must (1) define the task, (2) select, (3) locate, and (4) use appropriate information sources; (5) pull the information together; and, (6) decide that the task is, in fact, complete. We don't want to leave success to chance or serendipity. We don't want students to experience frustration and task avoidance. We do want students to know the requirements and actions of each Big6 stage and the entire process so that they have a system to fall back on when they are having difficulty.

Level 3: The 12 Sub-Skills of the Big6™

Through research, experience, and careful diagnosis, each of the six skills can be subdivided into two sub-skills, (sometimes referred to as the "Little12"). These 12 component skills provide a more specific breakdown of the overall process and allow for focused design and development of instruction.

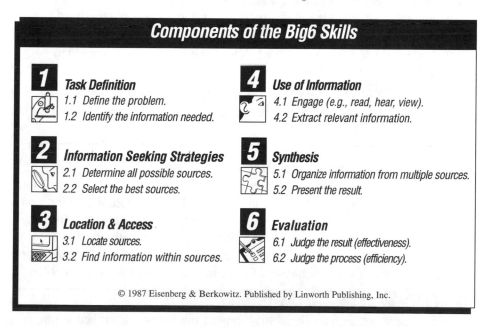

Components of the Big6 Skills

1 Task Definition
1.1 Define the problem.
1.2 Identify the information needed.

2 Information Seeking Strategies
2.1 Determine all possible sources.
2.2 Select the best sources.

3 Location & Access
3.1 Locate sources.
3.2 Find information within sources.

4 Use of Information
4.1 Engage (e.g., read, hear, view).
4.2 Extract relevant information.

5 Synthesis
5.1 Organize information from multiple sources.
5.2 Present the result.

6 Evaluation
6.1 Judge the result (effectiveness).
6.2 Judge the process (efficiency).

© 1987 Eisenberg & Berkowitz. Published by Linworth Publishing, Inc.

Though there is no requirement to address the Big6 components in any particular order, it is often useful to define the task before attempting to do anything else. After all, unless we know what we are expected to do, understand the nature and parameters of the problem, and can identify the information sources that will help us solve it, there is little chance for success. We would be remiss if we did not lead by example. The following sections will explain Task Definition in more detail and will provide specific examples.

Task Definition refers to the information need or the problem to be solved. Task Definition is the ability to determine the purpose and need for information.

> **Task Definition:**
> **1.1 Define the problem.**
> **1.2 Identify the information needed.**

1.1 Define the Problem

What is the problem to be solved? This is the initial question that students must answer in order to solve an information problem. Defining the parameters of what is required is the key to beginning the process. How the information problem is initially defined will determine the kinds of solutions or decisions to be considered throughout the process.

Examples of Task Definition 1.1

- Students demonstrate the ability to determine what is required in an assignment.
- Students demonstrate the ability to know that information is needed to complete the assignment.
- Students demonstrate the ability to select, narrow, or broaden topics.
- Students demonstrate the ability to formulate questions based on topics and subtopics.

1.2 Identify the information requirements of the problem

What information is needed in order to solve the problem or make the decision? It is necessary to diagnose the information needs before proceeding to the next skill so that maximum benefits are derived from the effort to collect information. Gathering too much information is as undesirable as gathering too little information. Once the parameters of the problem are determined, it is necessary to decide on the kinds and quantity of information that will solve the problem.

Examples of Task Definition 1.2:

- Students demonstrate the ability to pick out keywords embedded in a question or assignment.
- Students demonstrate the ability to recognize that the homework assignment requires factual information from at least three library sources.
- Students demonstrate the ability to determine statements that require evidence for support.
- Students demonstrate the ability to recognize the need to gather information from people through the use of an interview, survey, or questionnaire.

Task Definition is the stage at which students determine what needs to be done and what information is needed to get the job done. We find that the number one problem situation students can have is not knowing what's expected of them. There are lots of reasons for this (e.g., students not paying attention, teacher not clear, task is confusing). Regardless of the reason, if students don't understand what they are to do and don't understand the basis upon which their work will be graded, they are at a tremendous disadvantage.

Teachers can help with Task Definition by bringing the task and the criteria for assessment and grading into focus. Look at your assignments—is it clear what you are asking? Do the students truly understand? If not, we need to find ways to ensure that students do understand. Most of the time, teachers do give some form of direction concerning an assignment. We write the instructions on the board, discuss verbally what we want, or give out an assignment handout. But, communication about the task is mostly one-way and informational (making sure students have the information) rather than instructional (helping students to learn how to define tasks, zero in on critical aspects, and determine how they will fulfill the assignment at an appropriate level). Explaining an assignment is about as far as most teachers go. The assumption is that students will then know what to do and how to do it. Right? Wrong! Don't assume anything! We've found that often students in the intermediate and higher grades really don't understand what is meant by such aspects of assignments as:

- Compare and contrast
- Cite your sources
- Summarize
- Choose among
- Outline
- Describe.

We must provide integrated Big6-subject area opportunities for students to: learn effective and efficient ways to size up a task; understand what is being asked of them; and, determine the nature and types of information they need to complete the task.

One way to do this is to teach Task Definition when giving students an assignment. For example, give the students the assignment and offer two or three samples of completed work for the assignment including one sample that is definitely poor, virtually a parody of the assignment. Have the students assess the samples in terms of the assignment:

- Does it do what was required?
- Is it complete?
- How could it be improved?

Another technique is to give less rather than more direction on assignments. Teachers often lead students through every step in an assignment-verbally or in writing. Sometimes it is necessary for teachers to be very directive and specific, but too often this is done without even thinking of the message being communicated. When teachers give a great deal of detail or step-by-step directions, they are doing most of the Task Definition work. They are assuming primary responsibility for Task Definition. We want students to assume ownership and responsibility. Therefore, sometimes teachers should provide less rather than more explanation.

For example, don't spell out much detail at all, or make it a game. Just give a vague, broad description of what you want the students to do on a project, homework, or even for a test. Be willing to answer any and all questions about the assignment, but put the burden on the students to find out exactly what is expected. We remind students that they need to "get inside their teachers' heads" to figure out exactly what the teacher has in mind. They need to do "brain surgery" on their teachers—without actually opening up the skull! If they don't work it out, the students will suffer the consequences.

Part of the learning process is learning how to ask good questions. When you limit the details of the assignment, you open up opportunities for your students to ask for clarification, to check for understanding, to gauge whether their approach to the problem meets your expectations. There is another benefit—one that relates to teachers and good teaching. This kind of interactive communication helps teachers keep track of where students are having trouble or where they are finding the work too easy. They can revise the requirements as needed to adjust for errors in their underlying assumptions about what students already know. Based on problematic assumptions, teachers can go back and re-teach without throwing the assignment away. So, help your students and yourself—by giving little or no direction!

The second part to Task Definition (1.2) calls for identifying the information needed and determining the information requirements of an assignment. Here, we're not talking about various sources (books, computer databases, and magazines). The sources come later. In 1.2, we want students to think about what types of information they will need to get the job done (facts, opinions, pictures, and numerical information) and about how much information they will need.

The type of information problem and the way students define the task will suggest to them the kinds of information they will need. This in turn will suggest to students how they can find the information. This is an exercise "in gathering" all possible sources and sorting and selecting the best sources for the task at hand. This next section will describe the Big6 stage of "Information Seeking Strategies" and offer examples of how this stage furthers the information problem-solving process.

Information Seeking Strategies refers to determining the alternative information sources available that are appropriate to the information need. It's a mind-expanding stage that encourages students to think broadly and creatively.

> **Information Seeking Strategies:**
> **2.1 Determine all possible sources.**
> **2.2 Select the best sources.**

2.1 Determine the range of possible sources

What are all possible sources of information? Determining the universe of information sources appropriate to solving the information problem is an essential step after clarifying the task at hand. Knowledge of sources as well as imagination and creativity are important to successfully completing the step of determining likely sources.

Examples of Information Seeking Strategies 2.1:

- Students demonstrate the ability to generate a list of potential information sources, text and human, for a given information problem.

- Students demonstrate the ability to determine that an experiment is the appropriate way to gather information for a question about ecology.

- Students demonstrate the ability to recognize various Internet capabilities (e.g., World Wide Web, e-mail, Q&A services) as valuable resources.

- Students demonstrate the ability to ask the library media specialist if there are any good Web sources for information about space exploration.

- Students demonstrate the ability to identify electronic sources (e.g., CD-ROM, online databases).

2.2 Select the best sources

What are the best possible information sources—in a particular situation and at a certain point in time? This is the key question in 2.2. It is not only important to determine the range of sources, but it is vital to examine the sources to select those that are most likely to provide quality information to meet the task as defined.

Examples of Information Seeking Strategies 2.2:

- Students demonstrate the ability to decide that the *National Geographic* CD-ROM is the perfect source to complete the homework assignment.

- Students demonstrate the ability to decide that a segment from a current PBS program is a better source of information about whales than a magazine article from ten years ago.

- Students demonstrate the ability to assess the value of online discussion groups in relation to their task.
- Students demonstrate the ability to select sources that are suitable to meet the information need (e.g., current, authoritative, understandable, useful, available).

Once students understand the task or problem and have some idea about the types of information needed, their attention must turn to the range of possible information sources. This is the stage when students examine the possible information sources, and then select the sources that are most appropriate and available. Once they get into it, students are generally quite good at brainstorming sources. The goal is to get them to think broadly.

For example, when starting a report or project, students tend to rely on the usual sources—books, reference materials, and magazines. There are other sources that they generally overlook. These neglected sources include local and regional topic experts, historical societies, computer sources, and documentary films. Students might greatly enhance their projects by consulting these sources. Students must first think broadly about all types of sources. They must then narrow and select those sources that really meet their needs in terms of richness of information and availability. Brainstorm and narrow—these are critical thinking skills that can be developed with students of all ages.

Teachers can build various brainstorming activities into their classroom to help students identify the wide range of possible sources. For example, break the students into small groups and have each group brainstorm and narrow related to a topic, then compare results with the whole class. Or present an assignment and a list of possible sources. Then, on a card, have each student write down their source of choice and their reason for selecting that source.

Identifying the range of all possible sources and even selecting the best sources can be fun, but it is not very helpful for solving a problem unless the students are able to actually retrieve the information they need. The Big6 recognizes this dilemma by requiring that students have the skills to locate and access information. That's the next stage of the Big6.

3 | Location & Access

Location & Access refers to finding and retrieving information sources as well as specific information within sources.

> **Location & Access:**
> **3.1 Locate sources.**
> **3.2 Find information within sources.**

3.1 Locate sources

This is the stage where students find the sources physically or electronically. They need to determine where the sources are located—in the classroom, library, or some other place? How are the sources organized in those places—alphabetically by topic or author, by the Dewey Decimal classification system, not at all? Are there electronic tools for access such as an online catalog or is the information itself available on the Web or some other electronic format? And, if the source is a person, can they be reached by telephone or e-mail, or is it best (or necessary) to meet them in person?

Examples of Location & Access 3.1:

- Students demonstrate the ability to locate sources in the library.
- Students demonstrate the ability to use various Web search engines.
- Students demonstrate the ability find sources by Dewey Decimal number.
- Students demonstrate the ability to find resources throughout their community.
- Students demonstrate the ability to arrange to interview a key civic leader.

3.2 Find information within sources

This stage refers to actually getting to the information in a given source. Once the source is located, students must find the specific information they need. This isn't the most glamorous of skills, but it is essential nevertheless. And, there is a key to this stage—it's learning to search for and then use...the INDEX! This is the librarian's secret weapon—the index. Librarians and teachers have traditionally taught students about indexes, but doing so within the Big6 process makes a lot more sense to children.

Examples of Location & Access 3.2:

- Students demonstrate the ability to use the index in their textbook.
- Students demonstrate the ability to use a table of contents.
- Students demonstrate the ability to look up locations on a map.
- Students use a search tool in an electronic encyclopedia to get to the needed section.
- Students demonstrate the ability to skim to find the appropriate material on a website.
- Students use various finding tools on a website.

Location & Access should be the easiest stage, but it often isn't. It's also not a very exciting or particularly interesting stage. But, it does need to be completed if your children are to succeed. The goal in this stage is to locate the sources selected under the Information Seeking Strategies stage, and then actually to get to the information in those sources. In the past, librarians and teachers spent a great deal of time on this part of the process. That's changing because they realize that Location & Access is only part of the overall process.

Again, a crucial tool that can save lots of time in Location & Access of sources is an index. Indexes of various kinds (yellow pages, directories in shopping malls, back-of-the-book indexes, online magazine databases) make it easier to find information. Indexes may not be exciting, but they really do save time and effort. Students should always be on the lookout for indexes and they should know how to use them. Of course, indexes aren't the only way to locate and access information. Sometimes we just browse through the shelves, skim a book, or surf the Internet!

Teachers can help their students with Location & Access in lots of ways. For example, they can help in math by teaching how to search the textbook or class notes for examples of how to solve a type of problem. Or, they can demonstrate by example by using a back-of-the-book index while the children watch. Just recognizing "indexes" is a valuable lesson. Have students keep a log for one week of every time they use an index—what, why, how, and how useful was it?

Once students find the information, they need to know that it is appropriate to the task, and they need to be able to use it effectively. This aspect of completing a project can frustrate students' ultimate success because they have their own set of assumptions (e.g. about expectations, usefulness of information, clarity of instruction) that get in the way of effectively using the materials they found. The Big6 tackles this aspect of student learning by focusing them on engaging the information and extracting what's really relevant. That's the next stage—#4, Use of Information.

4   Use of Information

Use of Information refers to the application of information to meet defined information tasks.

> **Use of Information**
> **4.1 Engage (e.g., read, hear, view).**
> **4.2 Extract relevant information.**

4.1 Engage (e.g., read, hear, view) the information in a source
What information does the source provide? Ultimately, to gain useful and meaningful information from a source, students need to read, listen, or view the information in some form. We call these actions "engaging" the information and it is crucially important. The widespread emphasis on reading and its role in overall achievement attests to the importance of this stage.

Examples of Use of Information 4.1:
- Students demonstrate the ability to listen and comprehend.
- Students demonstrate the ability to watch a television news show and recognize relevant information.
- Students demonstrate the ability to conduct an interview—in person or via e-mail.
- Students demonstrate the ability to read and understand various forms of graphs.
- Students demonstrate the ability to interact with a Web site.

4.2 Extract information from a source

What specific information is worth applying to the task? This is determining "relevance" and can only be determined when students read, listen, or watch effectively. Even when students do locate sources and find appropriate information, they must be able to read and understand, or listen effectively, or watch for key concepts and examples relevant to their task. Otherwise, the source will not help them meet their information need. Extraction also involves taking the information with you in some way. This can include note taking, copying and pasting, downloading, filming or recording, or sometimes just remembering.

Examples of Use of Information 4.2:

- Students demonstrate the ability to list the key points in an article, chapter, or website related to a specific question or topic.
- Students demonstrate the ability to underline or highlight the topic statement from a magazine article on the technological revolution.
- Students demonstrate the ability to summarize concisely.
- Students demonstrate the ability to copy and paste information from a Web page or electronic resource—and to correctly cite the source.
- Students demonstrate the ability to download clip art.
- Students demonstrate the ability to properly cite information from any type of information source.

The previous Big6 stage, Location & Access, is easy compared to actually making use of the information found in the sources. This requires students to read, view, or listen; to decide what's important for the particular task at hand; and finally to extract the needed information. This isn't always easy to do, and can be quite time consuming.

Classroom teachers and teacher-librarians already do a great deal to develop Use of Information skills. For example, lessons and exercises on reading, viewing, or listening for a purpose, comprehension, and note-taking all help students to develop their ability to recognize and extract relevant information. What's sometimes missing is context, i.e., helping students to make the connection between these Use of Information actions and their place within the overall information problem-solving process.

Teachers and librarians can also focus various ways to skim or scan—in print or electronically—and then show students how to "capture" that information for use in their own work. The Web, online databases, digital and video cameras, cassette recorders, and other technological tools provide new ways for students to capture and use information. Of course, there is greater potential than ever before for the misrepresentation of work as their own. Therefore, another key component of Use of Information is to help students learn that properly crediting authors and sources from all types of formats is essential. We can also help students learn efficient ways to properly cite and credit.

Putting a project together or completing an assignment is a lot like baking a cake—once all the separate ingredients are identified, extraneous items put aside, and the relevant ingredients ordered and handled correctly, they need to be combined. Synthesis is the fifth stage of the Big6. This is the point when students pull together the information and begin to create the final project. Today, we have powerful new technology tools for Synthesis—from word processing to desktop publishing to multimedia and Web authoring. Therefore, Synthesis includes instruction on using these tools while at the same time going beyond the glitz to focus on developing good techniques and skills for organizing and presenting information in writing, graphic, and oral forms.

5 Synthesis

Synthesis refers to the integration and presentation of information from a variety of sources to meet the information need as defined.

> **Synthesis:**
> **5.1 Organize information from multiple sources.**
> **5.2 Present the result.**

5.1 Organize information from multiple sources

The key question in Synthesis is "How does the information from all of the sources fit together?" This skill focuses on determining the best ways to pull together, integrate, and organize the information to meet the task.

Examples of Synthesis 5.1:

- Students demonstrate the ability to create chronological timelines and charts relating key dates and events.
- Students demonstrate the ability to organize different pieces of information in different formats into a logical whole.
- Students demonstrate the ability to use word processing to revise the sequence, flow or outline of content in a paper, report, or project.
- Students demonstrate the ability to combine information from a range of print and electronic sources and from their own notes.
- Students demonstrate the ability to arrange and rearrange information using *PowerPoint* or other multimedia presentation software to arrange information.

5.2 Present information

How is the information best presented? What are the choices for presentation (e.g., written, graphic, oral, and multimedia) and how are those choices completed?

- Students demonstrate the ability to make a speech using multimedia or graphic presentation aids.
- Students demonstrate the ability to represent a still life in different media.
- Students demonstrate the ability to use *PowerPoint* or other multimedia presentation software.
- Students demonstrate the ability to create and label maps or other representations of geographic information.
- Students demonstrate the ability to graph data collected during a science experiment using electronic spreadsheets or other tools.
- Students demonstrate the ability to properly cite Web or other electronic sources in context and in bibliographies.

Synthesis involves organizing and presenting the information—putting it all together to complete a defined task. Sometimes Synthesis can be as simple as relaying a specific fact (as in answering a short-answer question) or making a decision (deciding on a topic for a report, a product to buy, an activity to join). At other times, Synthesis can be very complex and can involve the use of several sources, a variety of media or presentation formats, and the effective communication of abstract ideas.

Computer applications can help students organize and present information. Word processing, graphics programs, desktop publishing, databases, spreadsheets, and presentation packages can all help students put information together and present it effectively. Teachers don't have to be experts with any of these tools in order to help students learn to use them effectively. Teachers can arrange for librarians, technology teachers, or even expert students to help students learn the capabilities and features of a program. But, the important aspects are still the same regardless of tool or format:

- Use information to draw conclusions
- Form judgments based on evidence
- Create a logical argument
- Organize and communicate in a way that makes sense
- Draw conclusions
- Present a coherent whole.

Throughout the information problem-solving process, students should reflect on where they are and how they are doing. Students need to figure out where they are in the project or assignment, whether they are making progress toward its completion, how good it is, and how well they are using the available time. This is Evaluation, Big6 stage #6. But Evaluation is not meant to just be the final action that students take—a summary at the end. Evaluation is an activity that students need to get in the habit of doing all the time.

6 | Evaluation

In the Big6, evaluation refers to judgments on two different matters: (1) the degree to which the information problem is solved, and (2) the information problem-solving process itself.

> **Evaluation:**
> **6.1 Judge the result (effectiveness).**
> **6.2 Judge the process (efficiency).**

6.1 Judge the result

Is the task completed; is the problem resolved? This is the primary concern in Evaluation. While working on an assignment, students should routinely monitor their own progress. Sometimes, they might realize that they don't quite understand the task, and that they need to go back and change or adjust the task. Students must also be able to recognize that they are done and that the quality of the result is at the level they (and their teacher) desire. One important way that students can accomplish this "summative evaluation" is to compare their resulting product, paper, or report (or other form of assignment) to clearly understood criteria. However, at the secondary level, determining and establishing criteria is not the sole responsibility of the teachers. Students skilled in the Big6 should be able to recognize criteria and assess their own success.

Examples of Evaluation 6.1:

- Students demonstrate the ability to evaluate multimedia presentations for both content and format.
- Students demonstrate the ability to determine whether they are on the right track in science labs and experiments.
- Students demonstrate the ability to judge the effectiveness of three different forms of information products (e.g., T.V. show, electronic database, website, book).
- Students demonstrate the ability to rate their projects based on a set of criteria that they set themselves.

6.2 Judge the information problem-solving process

For students to continue to improve their information problem-solving abilities, they need to learn how to assess their actions. They should also consider how they can be more efficient—in terms of saving time and effort—in carrying out each component skill.

- Students demonstrate the ability to set criteria for quality literary criticism papers.
- Students demonstrate the ability to assess their confidence in taking AP history practice tests.
- Students demonstrate the ability to thoughtfully consider how well they were able to use electronic sources throughout their project.
- Students demonstrate the ability to compare the amount of time that they estimate should be spent on an assignment with the actual amount of time spent.
- Students demonstrate the ability to reflect on their level of personal effort and time spent during their work on the assignment.

In the Evaluation stage, students should reflect on the process and result of their work. Are they pleased with what they are doing or have completed? If they could do the project again, what might they do differently? Evaluation determines the effectiveness and efficiency of the information problem-solving process. Effectiveness is another way of saying, how good is the product? What grade are you likely to get? Efficiency refers to time and effort. If the children were to do the work again, how could they do as well, but save some time and effort?

It's important to get students to reflect on their performance. They need to think about their result and decide if they are pleased with it. It's not always necessary to get a top grade; sometimes "okay" is enough. At other times, they should want to strive for excellence. Students need to understand and recognize the difference. They also need to think about the process. Where did they get stuck? Where did they waste time? All this so they can make changes next time. These kinds of self-reflection actions are true learning experiences. When students are self-aware, they evaluate themselves and can change their behavior for the better in the future.

There are a number of strategies that teachers can use to focus students' attention on Evaluation. For example, provide "time-out" reflection points during the process to assess how well they are doing, if they are clear about the assignment, and where in the process are they having difficulties. Have students keep a log during an assignment and later discuss steps taken, successes, and areas for improvement. When completing major assignments, ask students to include a one-page "process review" piece in which they discuss their activities, successes and concerns, and how they might improve in the future.

Teachers can also provide clear directions and criteria for assessment. This doesn't mean being over-detailed or laborious. It means making sure that students understand what they are being asked to do and how they will be graded.

Scoring guides or rubrics are another way to help students assess themselves or fully understand how they will be assessed. Ultimately, evaluation should encourage students to improve and help them to do so. Classroom teachers and teacher-librarians can work with students on identifying what was the most difficult aspect of an assignment and what they might do differently next time.

Evaluation activities are not just for the end of the process. Teachers can coach students to reflect during each stage of the information problem-solving process. In designing instruction, plan for frequent opportunities to check for understanding and progress. Also be available to help trouble-shoot when problems arise. These are not just content or subject comprehension problems, but problems in relation to the process, in terms of what to do next or how to proceed.

And finally to reinforce an earlier point, a goal in secondary schools is to reinforce students' abilities to assess themselves. Students' self-assessments should be similar to those of their teachers. One technique is to have students estimate their grades before handing in an assignment. Also ask, "if you had more time, what would you do differently and why?" The students don't have to go back and actually make the changes; just recognizing how they would do something differently reflects substantive learning.

In Evaluation, we want to encourage students to gauge their own growth, progress, strengths, and skills in a way that is useful to their continued learning. Evaluation is the culmination of the entire process, but it is often the part of the process that receives the least attention. Teachers and librarians should carefully consider activities and exercises to emphasize Evaluation. In doing so, they actually help students in every one of the Big6 skills.

Summary

This chapter offered an extensive view of the Big6 process and the specifics of the Big6 Skills. The next chapter directly addresses the issue of technology. Considering technology and technology tools within the Big6 process provides students with a powerful context for becoming effective and efficient users of information.

Reflections

CHAPTER 3

Technology with a Big6™ Face

Introduction

"Students must be proficient in using computer technology."

This is a clear goal in K-12 education today, and schools world-wide are scrambling to improve the level of computer technology in schools as well as to infuse computer technology into the instructional program. These efforts are impressive in terms of the numbers of computers, the installation of networks, and the level and speed of Internet connectivity.

It's also encouraging to note a growing realization that being computer literate is more than simply being able to operate a computer. First, there is recognition that it's not just computers that we want students to be able to use. We want them to be literate in using the full range of information technologies—productivity tools, communications capabilities, information resources and systems, hand-held devices, and more. Second, the focus is shifting from "teaching computing in a separate class located in a computer lab" to "students learning to use the full range of information technology for a purpose as part of the subject area curriculum."

We want students to know more than a particular set of commands or even how to use a particular type of software. We want students to use technology flexibly and creatively. We want them to be able to size up a task, recognize how technology might help them to fulfill the task, and then use the technology to do so.

Helping students learn to apply technology in these ways requires a change in the way computer skills are traditionally taught in school. It means moving from teaching isolated "computer skills" to teaching integrated "information and technology skills." Integration means infusing technology in the curriculum, but equally importantly, it means infusing technology into each stage of the Big6 information problem-solving process. The Big6 provides the framework for learning and applying technology. Individual information and technology skills take on new meaning when they are integrated within the Big6, and students develop true "computer literacy" because they have genuinely applied various computer and technology skills as part of the learning process.

Moving from teaching isolated computer skills to helping students learn integrated information and technology skills is not just a good idea—it's essential if we are to put students in a position to succeed in an increasingly complex and changing world. Peter Drucker, well-known management guru, stated that "executives have become computer-literate . . . but not many executives are information literate'"" (*Wall Street Journal*, Dec. 1, 1992, p.A16). In our view, Drucker is saying that being able to use computers is not enough. Executives must be able to apply computer skills to real situations and needs. Executives must be able to identify information problems and be able to locate, use, synthesize, and evaluate information in relation to those problems. These are the same skill needs that exist for all people living in an information society.

There are many good reasons for moving from teaching isolated computer skills to teaching integrated information and technology skills. Technology is changing at a breath-taking pace and will continue to do so for the foreseeable future. In a speech at the 1997 National Educational Computing Conference in Seattle, Bill Gates stated that computing power has increased 1 million times over the past 20 years and will likely do so again in the next 20 years!

A million times more powerful!! Will learning isolated specific skills such as keyboarding, word processing, or even World Wide Web searching suffice? Clearly not. Will learning to use whatever technologies come along to boost our abilities within the overall information problem-solving process suffice? Absolutely.

That's what it means to look at technology from a Big6 perspective; to give technology a Big6 face.

Technology and the Big6™

It's actually relatively easy to view technology from a Big6 perspective.

Let's take a typical basic technology—"a pencil and paper." In Big6 terms, how can a pencil and paper help us to be more productive? Clearly, a pencil and paper boosts our ability to synthesize, organize, and present information (Big6 #5).

What are the electronic equivalents of a pencil and paper—the tools that help us even more to synthesize? Clearly, there's word processing. There's also desktop publishing, word processing, desktop publishing, and *HyperStudio, PowerPoint* and other presentation software programs. All these are used to organize and present information, Big6 #5.

Here's another basic technology—"a phone book." The phone book is an aid for Big6 #3—Location & Access. What are the electronic technology equivalents to the phone book? There are the online or CD-ROM bibliographic databases, Web browsers and search engines (e.g., Yahoo!, Lycos, go.com).

Other technologies can be viewed in this way. Similar to books, full-text databases, CD-ROM encyclopedias, and other electronic resources are part of an effective Information Seeking Strategy (Big6 #2) and are read/viewed/listened-to for information (Big6 #4). When a face-to-face meeting isn't possible, e-mail is highly useful for linking students with their teachers or with other students for Task Definition activities (Big6 #1), and later for Evaluation (Big6 #6). And more and more students are learning to take notes and extract information by using the copy and paste functions in word processing software.

When integrated into the information problem-solving process, these technological capabilities become powerful information tools for students. Figure 3.1 provides a summary of how some of today's technologies fit within the Big6 process.

Figure 3.1: *Computer Capabilities and the Big6™*

Word processing	SYNTHESIS (writing) USE OF INFORMATION (note-taking)
Spell/grammar checking	EVALUATION
Desktop publishing	SYNTHESIS
Presentation/Multimedia software	SYNTHESIS
Electronic spreadsheets	SYNTHESIS
Online library catalog	LOCATION & ACCESS
Electronic magazine index	LOCATION & ACCESS USE OF INFORMATION
Full-text electronic resources	INFORMATION SEEKING STRATEGIES USE OF INFORMATION
Brainstorming software	TASK DEFINITION
Copy-paste (in various programs)	USE OF INFORMATION

Examples of Technology in Big6™ Contexts

Integrating technology instruction with the Big6 provides a context for technology skills instruction. It also helps students learn to apply technology flexibly and creatively.

In Chapter 4, we explain the importance of two contexts—the Big6 process and the subject area classroom curriculum—to effective Big6 Skills instruction. This is particularly true for teaching technology skills. We avoid teaching technology skills in isolation when we combine them with the Big6 process and with real subject area curriculum and assignments.

For example, a 9th grade class is studying regions of the Far East and comparing various features (e.g., geography, population, industry, and special attributes). The assignment is to create a comparative chart that highlights differences and similarities.

As students go through the work for the assignment, they engage in various stages of the Big6. The teacher recognizes that this might be a good opportunity to teach technology and the Big6. She arranges with the library media specialist for the students to learn about electronic searching for books in various electronic resources (Big6 #3, Location & Access). The students will also search on the World Wide Web and compare what they found in terms of quality, amount of information, and time and effort.

The teacher also speaks to the technology teacher about possible programs to help the students create charts (Big6 #5, Synthesis). The technology teacher recommends a draw/paint program and schedules the class for a special lesson.

This is a powerful example of the integration of technology, the Big6, and curriculum. Students are learning to use technology as part of the information problem-solving process to perform better in classroom curriculum.

An English class is studying American Literature. Working in groups, the students are to create a formal report on the historical context of a novel that they selected. The students brainstorm possible sources and one group decides that talking to someone who is an expert in history and American literature is a good idea; perhaps this person is teaching at a university (Big6 #2, Information Seeking Strategies). However, they realize they have no way of getting to a university or anywhere else by themselves (Big6 #3, Location & Access). Their teacher suggests they send an electronic message or e-mail to the library media specialist asking what to do. They do so and she suggests conducting the interview through the Internet, either by e-mail or chat.

But, where can they find a likely university and the e-mail address of someone there who teaches this subject (Big6 #3, Location & Access)? The students realize they can use a Web search engine to locate various universities, which probably include lists of staff.

Over the next few days, the students make contact with a university professor who agrees to answer their questions via e-mail. The students e-mail the questions and are excited when they get a response in three days. They copy and paste from the e-mail into a word processing document and note the name of their contact, e-mail address, and dates of the e-mail exchanges.

Technologies incorporated in this example include the use of a messaging or e-mail program, Web search engine, Web browser, and word processing program. The copy-paste function from e-mail is also an important skill for the students to learn. Another twist to this assignment would be to use multimedia presentation software to create and present the report instead of the traditional written format (Big6 #5, Synthesis).

When we reflect on integrating technology skills into teaching and learning, we realize that it is not necessary to change the fundamentals of quality instruction or the information problem-solving perspective that is at the heart of the Big6 Skills approach. The implementation of technology through the Big6 works in the following ways:

- Develops students' problem-solving, complex thinking, and information management abilities.
- Enables students to become comfortable with technology and understand that the technologies are valuable tools to help them perform their work.
- Focuses students' attention on using technologies as tools to extend knowledge and to individualize learning.
- Develops an active participatory learning process in which students become self-directed learners.
- Facilitates integrating technology across all grades and into all disciplines.
- Assists teachers to change their roles from presenters of information to "learning coaches" who offer tools and advice.
- Helps teachers introduce technology and have students use technologies even if the teachers aren't experts themselves.

Implementing technology within the Big6 process is easy, direct, and powerful. It also encourages classroom teachers, library media specialists, and technology teachers to collaboratively design instruction that can intentionally create challenging and exciting learning experiences. Such opportunities expand the scope of new technology use by all students.

The Big6™ and the Internet

The Internet provides an overwhelming set of technologies that deserve special note. The World Wide Web, in particular, provides unprecedented access to information, along with some serious challenges. For the first time in history, we have immediate access to massive amounts of information. The sheer volume is mind-boggling. One study by NEC Research Institute and Inktomi Corporation estimates that the Web had 320 million pages in December 1997, 820 million pages by February 1999, and more than 1 billion in February of 2000. Compare this to 18 million published works in the Library of Congress (Glanz, 2000).

At the same time, we constantly hear that yes, there is so much information on the Web, but also that it's so hard to find what you want on the Web. How do you make sense of it all? How do you really use it effectively and efficiently?

Again, we fall back on the Big6 process. To make sense of the Web involves most of the Big6 process—from Task Definition to Evaluation. Figure 3.2 shows how Internet and Web capabilities fit within the Big6 context. All stages of the Big6 can benefit from use of the Internet and Web.

Figure 3.2: *Internet Capabilities and the Big6™*

E-mail, chat, messaging (ICQ)	TASK DEFINITION INFORMATION SEEKING STRATEGIES LOCATION & ACCESS USE OF INFORMATION SYNTHESIS EVALUATION
Mailing lists (listservs), newsgroups, chat	TASK DEFINITION INFORMATION SEEKING STRATEGIES LOCATION & ACCESS USE OF INFORMATION SYNTHESIS EVALUATION
Web browsers (Netscape, Internet Explorer)	INFORMATION SEEKING STRATEGIES LOCATION & ACCESS
Search engines (Yahoo!, Hotbot, Lycos, Excite, Alta Vista)	INFORMATION SEEKING STRATEGIES LOCATION & ACCESS
Portals (My Yahoo!, MSN, AOL)	INFORMATION SEEKING STRATEGIES LOCATION & ACCESS USE OF INFORMATION
Web authoring (HTML)	SYNTHESIS
Websites	USE OF INFORMATION

Here are some Big6 suggestions for using the Web in teaching:

Task Definition: Don't start with the Web; start with the problem. Discuss what the students are trying to accomplish and what the result might look like.

Information Seeking Strategies: Consider options and alternatives—even within the Web. Big6 #2.1 involves determining possibilities, #2.2 is to choose the best sources given the situation. That means applying criteria, such as closeness to the problem, accuracy, currency, and authority of each website. Students should be able to explain why they chose to use a particular website based on one or more of these criteria.

Location & Access: Search tools are a key! Discuss how the various search systems differ. Students should be able to explain why they prefer one over another.

Use of Information: This stage involves selecting good information, again based on applying criteria. Discuss criteria and how to make choices based on criteria.

Synthesis: Ease-of-use is the primary concern in Synthesis. How easy is it to find information on a website? Is it logical, easy-to-understand, simple to navigate, etc?

Evaluation: One aspect to focus on is efficiency—saving time and effort while maintaining quality. This relates directly to the original concern of not being overwhelmed by information. What are some strategies for using the Web for a purpose, but doing so without wasting considerable time?

We cannot overemphasize that the key for classroom, library, and technology teachers is not to focus on the Web or technology itself. We should focus on the learning goals, the content, and the Big6 process and then make the technology connection. For example, helping students become discriminating users of information—applying good judgment in selecting sources and information within sources—is central to the Big6 stages of Information Seeking Strategies and Use of Information. These essentials are transferable, long-term Big6 abilities. The way to help students gain these abilities is through integrating subject area-Big6-technology instruction.

Summary

This chapter provided a conceptual framework and approach for helping students learn and use technology in meaningful ways. Technologies can boost students' abilities to solve curriculum-based information problems. The key is to use technology within the Big6 process. Figure 3.3 presents the Big6 view and how various current technologies fit into the Big6.

The next chapter turns to the question of implementation. Teaching the Big6 and Web skills in context means determining when students actually are working on a project or assignment that lends itself to using the Web. Also, it's not necessary to cover all Big6 Skills in each context. For example, with one assignment, we might teach the Web and Task Definition; in a later unit we would emphasize Information Seeking Strategies or Evaluation. They key is to make the connection—to link students' learning about the Web into a relevant Big6 and curricular context.

When it comes to technology, we can't know it all or even anticipate what it might be. Remember the earlier quote from Bill Gates—in 20 years we will have computers that are a million times more powerful than those of today. No one really knows into what forms this capability will translate.

What we as educators can do is to ask the key questions with the Big6 in mind:

- What do we want to accomplish—from a content and a Big6 perspective?
- How can the technology help to do it?
- In our schools, classrooms, libraries, labs, and homes—what will it take to use the technology in this way?
- Will this use really make a difference for students—in terms effectiveness and efficiency?
- Is it worth taking the time and effort to integrate the technology instruction now?
- If yes, what will it take? How can we provide meaningful learning opportunities that integrate content, process, and technology.

Figure 3.3 *The Big6™ and Technology*

TASK DEFINITION	E-mail, group discussions (mailing lists, news groups), brainstorming software, chat (IRC, MOO, Palace), videoconferencing (CUSeeMe), groupware
INFO SEEKING STRATEGIES	Online catalogs, info retrieval, electronic resources (CD-ROMs, intranet), WWW/net resources, AskERIC[1], Internet Public Library[2], online discussion groups (mailing lists)
LOCATION & ACCESS	Online catalogs, electronic indexes, WWW browsers (Netscape[3]), search engines (Yahoo[4], Alta Vista[5], Lycos[6], Hotbot[7]), AskERIC, AskA+ Locator[8], telnet, ftp, e-mail
USE OF INFORMATION	Upload/download, word processing, copy-paste, outliners, spread-sheets, databases (for analysis of data), statistical packages
SYNTHESIS	Word processing, desktop publishing, graphics, spreadsheets, database management, hypermedia, presentation software, down/up load, ftp, e-journals, mailing lists, newsgroups, Web/HTML authoring
EVALUATION	Spell/grammar checkers, e-mail, online discussions (listservs, newsgroups), chat (IRC, MOO, Palace), videoconferencing (CUSeeMe), groupware

[1] *AskERIC—http://www.askeric.org*

[2] *Internet Public Library—http://www.ipl.org/*

[3] *Netscape—http://www.netscape.com/*

[4] *Yahoo—http://www.yahoo.com/*

[5] *AltaVista—http://www.altavista.com*

[6] *Lycos—http: www.lycos.com/*

[7] *Hotbot—http://hotbot.lycos.com/*

[7] *AskA+ Locator—http://www.vrd.org/locator/index.html*

Reflections

CHAPTER 4

Implementing the Big6:™ Context, Context, Context

Warning: Teaching Information & Technology Skills Out of Context is Hazardous to Your Students' Health.

Introduction: Contexts

In real estate, they talk about the three key elements: location, location, and location. We look at the key elements to implementing a meaningful Big6 information and technology skills program in a similar way: context, context, and context.

There are actually two essential contexts for successful Big6 Skills instruction: (1) the process itself and (2) real needs—either curricular or personal. When we talk about an integrated Big6 Skills program, we mean integrating Big6 learning and teaching in both of these contexts.

Another way to think of these contexts is as "anchors." When students are engaged in a task or solving a problem, it's easy to get lost. But, they are in a much better position to succeed if, at any point in time, they can identify the two anchors:

> **#1-Where are they in the Big6 process?**
> **#2-What's the curriculum or personal need?**

Let's look at each of these contexts in more detail.

Context 1: The Big6™ Process

As explained in Chapter 2, the Big6 is a process composed of six stages of skills. While successful information problem-solving requires completion of all stages, the stages do not need to be completed in any particular order or in any set amount of time. A stage can be repeated or revisited a number of times. And, sometimes a stage is completed with little effort, while at other times a stage is difficult and time consuming.

Knowing where they are in the process is very helpful for students. It helps them to know what's been completed and what is still to do. When working on an assignment, project, report, or even an information problem of personal interest, students should be able to identify where they are in the process. For example, are they reading an article related to current events? That's Use of Information, Big6 #4. Are they searching for sources using a CD-ROM index? That's Big6 #3, Location & Access.

Similarly, teachers should frame instructional and learning experiences related to information and technology skills instruction within the Big6 process. Are they teaching *PowerPoint* for multimedia presentation? That's Synthesis, Big6 #5. Are students working with the library media specialist to determine possible sources for a project? That's Information Seeking Strategies, Big6 #2.

Anchoring instruction in individual skills within the overall Big6 process provides students with a familiar reference point. They see the connections among seemingly separate skills and are able to reflect on what came before and anticipate what comes after.

Therefore, we recommend continually working with students to help them recognize where they are in the process. Some ways that teachers can do this is by

- Identifying for students the various Big6 stages as they go through an assignment, project, or report
- Using a story or video to point out the Big6 stages related to the actions of one or more characters
- Modeling Big6 process recognition by pointing out when they themselves are engaging in a particular Big6 stage, and
- Asking students, verbally or in writing, to identify which Big6 stage they are working on.

Context 2: Curriculum

Information is a pervasive and essential part of our society and our lives. We are, at our essence, processors and users of information. This is not a recent development. Humans have always been dependent upon information to help them make decisions and to guide their actions. The change has come in the sheer volume of information and the complexity of information systems—largely due to advances in information technology and the accelerated rate at which we live.

Information is pervasive, and so are the Big6 information skills. Therefore, there are many opportunities for teaching and learning the Big6 Skills. From research and experience, we know that the Big6 Skills are best learned in the context of real needs—school or personal. Students today, more than ever, want to see connections between what they are learning and their lives. They want to know how something is relevant. This is no problem for the Big6, as the approach emphasizes applicability across environments and situations.

Most often in school settings, the context for Big6 Skills instruction is the actual classroom curriculum. This includes the subject area units and lessons of study, and most importantly, the assignments on which students will be evaluated. Throughout the school year, teachers and students engage in a rich range of curriculum subjects and topics. In fact, one of the current problems we face in education is "curriculum information overload"—there's just too much to cover in a limited time.

That's why, in implementing Big6 instruction, we do not promote adding new curriculum content, units, or topics. There's plenty going on in the curriculum already. The last thing that classroom teachers and students need is more content. Therefore, from a Big6 perspective, the challenge is to determine good opportunities for learning and teaching Big6 Skills within the existing curriculum. This involves taking the following actions:

(1) Analyze the curriculum to (a) select units and assignments which are well-suited to Big6 Skills instruction, and (b) determine which Big6 Skills are particularly relevant to the selected curriculum units and assignments

(2) Develop a broad plan that links the Big6 to various curriculum units

(3) Design integrated unit and lesson plans to teach the Big6 in the context of the subject area curriculum.

We strongly advocate a collaborative approach to Big6 Skills instruction. That is, classroom teachers, library media specialists, technology teachers, and other educators can work together to analyze the curriculum, develop a broad plan, and design specific unit and lesson plans that integrate the Big6 and classroom content. These educators can also collaborate on teaching and assessment.

Analyzing Curriculum from a Big6™ Perspective

As stated above, effective Big6 instruction starts with selecting existing curriculum units which are best suited to integrated Big6 Skills instruction. We refer to these units as "big juicies"—those information-rich curriculum units that are filled and dripping with Big6 potential. "Big juicy" units are rich in information needs, resources, and processing. These are the units that offer particularly good opportunities for teaching specific Big6 Skills within the overall Big6 process.

For example, select units that involve a report, project, or product rather than those that rely on a test for assessment. Focus on units that require a range of multiple resources rather than only the textbook. Desirable units should also involve a large number of students and span a reasonable timeframe. Let's see how this might work in practice.

High school biology teacher, Ms. Lowe, and library media specialist, Mr. Bennett, meet to discuss how they might collaborate to help students improve their information problem-solving skills while they study biology. They analyze the major units that Ms. Lowe plans to teach during the school year, and agree that there are three key units because they (1) result in some form or product of project, (2) require lots of different types of resources, (3) involve the whole class, and (4) span more than just a week or two. In other words, these three units seem to be particularly "information-rich," and are perfect candidates for integrated biology-Big6 instruction. These are the big juicies:

- **The anatomy unit:** taught early in the school year, takes three weeks, involves significant use of the WWW, results in individual *PowerPoint*-supported oral presentations.

- **The circulatory system unit:** taught in the second marking period, takes two weeks, involves a series of worksheets that combine to make a study guide, also requires students to identify structures and functions, and to analyze the effect of oxygenation on various other systems (e.g. nervous system, immune system, digestive system).

- **The digestive system unit:** taught in the third marking period, results in group presentations on the digestive process in different animals, and usually involves extensive information seeking and searching.

What now? Do they select among these units or do they just integrate the Big6 with all three? Do they teach all the Big6 Skills with each unit or focus on specific Big6 Skills.

These choices depend upon other factors including the time available for Big6 instruction and what else is going on during the school year. We do, however, recommend that while they review and reinforce the overall Big6 process with each unit, Ms. Lowe and Mr. Bennett should provide targeted Big6 Skills instruction on one or two of the specific skills. For example:

- The anatomy unit relies on *PowerPoint* and the Web, so lessons can be taught on both. *PowerPoint* is a Synthesis tool, so that's a Big6 #5 lesson focusing on organizing and presenting principles using *PowerPoint*. Lessons on the Web might focus on identifying useful types of websites (Information Seeking Strategies, Big6 #2), using keyword search terms (Location & Access, Big6 #3), and recognizing and extracting relevant information, (Use of Information, Big6 #4).

- The circulatory system unit might be a good unit in which to focus on Task Definition, (Big6 #1) since each worksheet has a different focus. There's also a great deal of targeted analysis, so Use of Information, Big6 #4, is again important.

- The digestive system unit is a group project and comes later in the school year. This would be a good opportunity to review the entire Big6 process while emphasizing defining tasks and dividing up the work (Big6 #1, Task Definition) and how to put group presentations together so they make sense and flow easily (Big6 #5, Synthesis). Evaluation (Big6 #6) can also play a big role in group projects as students may be required to judge themselves and other group members or to assess the final products of other groups.

In actual school settings, selecting units for integrated Big6 instruction and overall Big6 Skills planning depends upon the specific needs of the students as well as the setting and situation. The ultimate goal is to provide frequent opportunities for students to learn and practice the Big6. Repetition is crucial. While these skills may seem to be simple or common sense at first, they actually are quite involved and can be difficult to master. We cannot overstress this point—we learn through repetition. It's not enough to teach each Big6 Skill or sub-skill once. Students' proficiency with specific Big6 Skills as well as the overall process will improve over time—if they have regular opportunities to learn and to apply the Big6.

Planning for Big6 learning will differ based upon the situation, curriculum, setting, and who is going to be involved, e.g., the classroom teacher, library media specialist, teaching team, technology teacher, entire grade level or subject area, school or district. Examples of each of these situations are presented below.

Planning and Plans for the Individual Teacher

Classroom teachers organize and plan the school year around a series of curriculum units and lessons. Based on local or state curriculum guides, teachers determine the sequence of units, their general goals and objectives, and the time they will spend on each unit. While they frequently make adjustments during the school year, most teachers try to cover the intended units in sequence.

As described above, we suggest that teachers review the existing curriculum plans to determine opportunities to integrate Big6 Skills instruction. The task is to first identify units that have good potential for integrating Big6 Skills and then decide which Big6 Skills to emphasize with each unit.

Units that are good candidates for integrating Big6 Skills instruction generally:

- Are of longer duration
- Involve a report, project, or product rather than a quiz or test
- Use multiple resources
- Involve a range of teaching methods.

As noted, it is not necessary or desirable to teach all stages of the Big6 with each curriculum unit. The Big6 is applicable to any problem-solving situation, so students will have ample opportunity to work on the Big6 throughout the school year. Therefore, when students are first presented with an assignment as part of a curriculum unit, we recommend first "talking through" the assignment in the context of the overall Big6 process. Then, as students work through the assignment, the teacher, often in partnership with the library media specialist and technology teacher, can offer more in-depth lessons on one or more of the Big6 Skills. By the end of the school year, students in the class should have experienced a full range of Big6 lessons in the context of the real curriculum and the overall Big6 process.

Figure 4.1 is a sample "Big6 Skills by Unit Matrix" for Mr. Robinson, a social studies teacher with classes in U.S. history and economics. The matrix is an efficient way to summarize Mr. Robinson's integrated Big6 plans. (Note: the plans included here are composites of a number of teachers and settings. They do not actually refer to any specific school, district, or teacher).

Figure 4.1 documents the units that Mr. Robinson intends to integrate with Big6 Skills instruction. The units are sorted chronologically in terms of marking period (M_Per) which notes the order they will be introduced in the school year. Information is also included on the grade level (GR; note that the economics class is open to both 11th and 12th graders), the subject, assignments, and Big6 Skills targeted for in-depth instruction. A large X indicates that a Big6 lesson will be taught while a small x indicates that the Big6 Skill will only be touched on.

For example, the first U. S. History unit is about Colonial America, and is taught in the first marking period. This is a textbook-based unit, and the assignments are introductory—a timeline and a test. The Big6 lesson relates to Big6 #4—Use of Information—focusing on effective and efficient use of textbook information. Mr. Hancock will also mention Big6 #1—Task Definition—by helping students to learn that it is their responsibility to ask about the scope and format of the test.

From Figure 4.1, we also see that Mr. Robinson uses the Industrial Revolution unit as a major kickoff to the Big6 process during the second marking periods. Here, he and the library media specialist will teach lessons on each of the Big6 as students go through the process. Mr. Robinson will also introduce technology skills within the Big6 process in the Industrial Revolution unit, particularly the use of the Web and other electronic resources, *PowerPoint* presentation software, and e-mail. Mr. Robinson returns to these integrated technology skills in the America Today unit at the end of the year.

In the economics class, Mr. Robinson covers the range of Big6 skills over five units. Each unit has a different assignment format—project, chart, test, report, and analysis and profile. This gives the students an opportunity to apply the Big6 in different ways. The stock market unit spans the entire year and focuses on competitive intelligence and strategic use of information.

Figure 4.1: *Big6™ Skills by Unit Matrix:*
Mr. Robinson–Social Studies Teacher

The Big6™

GR	UNIT	SUBJECT	ASSIGNMENT	M_PER	1	2	3	4	5	6	TECHNOLOGY	COMMENTS
11-12	Stock Market	Economics	project	1234	X	X	X	X	x	X	WWW, elec res	full-year, competitive intelligence
10-10	Colonial America	US History	timeline, test	1xxx	x			X				use of textbook
10-10	Industrial Revolution	US History	project	x2xx	X	X	X	X	X	X	WWW, elec res, word proc,	major reports–all Big6
11-12	Markets	Economics	chart–events	x2xx				X		X		focus on analysis
10-10	Woman's Suffrage	US History	report	xx3x		X	X				WWW	
10-10	Prosperity/Depression 20s & 30s	US History	audio project	xx3x	X			X	X		audio recording	groups do two radio news shows
11-12	Supply & Demand	Economics	test	xx3x	X							understand the test
11-12	Economics Institutions	Economics	report	xx3x	x	x	x	x	x	X	WWW, elec res, word proc	major project–Big6 focus printed or Web-based
10-10	America Today	US History	project	xxx4	X				X		WWW, elec res, word proc	
11-12	The New Information Economy	Economics	industry analysis and	xxx4	x	X	x	X	x	x	WWW, elec res, word proc, present, graphics, e-mail	

Students can really hone their evaluation of information skills in this unit. The final assignment, the industry profile, is a good summary assignment that will allow him to gauge the overall level of students' skills.

If developed at the beginning of the school year, the Big6 Skills by Unit Matrix becomes a blueprint for integrated information skills instruction. It can also be updated during the year to reflect what actually takes place. Therefore, at the end of the year, the matrix offers detailed documentation of what was actually accomplished. The plans also serve as the basis for follow-up planning by the teacher for the next year and for other teachers who will have the same students the next year.

Planning and Plans for a Subject Area, Grade, or Team

While Big6 implementation through individual teachers is essential, it is also valuable to coordinate Big6 Skills instruction in broader contexts. This section explains how this can happen within a particular subject area, grade, or team.

Figure 4.2 offers a sample Big6 Skills by Unit Matrix for a high school social studies department. The data included is similar to figure 1, however we have added columns for Teacher and Grade and were more specific in listing the course titles under Subject.

On the plan, we see that in the 9th grade, Ms. Sullivan (TJS), intends to focus on the Big6 in three units. In the first marking period, the class studies Latin America and the unit culminates in a test. Since this is the beginning of the school year, Ms. Sullivan will quickly review the overall Big6 process, but will develop lessons that focus on:

- Task Definition: understanding what is expected on her tests
- Synthesis: developing strategies for writing short essays on tests
- Evaluation: recognizing the criteria for success including which topics and concepts are more or less important.

Ms. Sullivan, the library media specialist, and technology teacher will deliver other Big6 lessons during the school year. For example, the library media specialist will provide a lesson about selecting, locating, and using quality information sources particularly in relation to the World Wide Web (Big6 #s 2,3,4) for the Northern Africa unit, and the technology teacher will offer instruction on special software for creating computer-generated maps (Big6 #5) for the unit on India.

The matrix documents similar intentions by other teachers. The plan for Mr. Robinson (ALR) was discussed in the previous section. Here, we can compare his plans to two other 10th grade teachers (Mr. Jackson, WAJ and Ms. Rossini, AAR). They have each used the Big6 with one unit in the past and are willing to expand to a second unit. Notice that the Civil War unit in Rossini's class will culminate in a report, allowing for developing Big6 Skills #2 through 4: Information Seeking Strategies, Location & Access, and Use of

Figure 4.2: Big6™ Skills by Unit Matrix: Secondary School
Social Studies Department Sorted by Grade and Teacher

The Big6™

GR	TCHR	UNIT	SUBJECT	ASSIGNMENT	M_PER	1	2	3	4	5	6	TECHNOLOGY	COMMENTS
07-07	TCH	Recycling	Social Studies	product	x23x	X	X	X	x	X	X	WWW, elec res, word proc, present, e-mail	lots of technology
08-08	CGR	Rainforest	Social Studies	test, short written assignment, project	1xxx			X	x			WWW, word proc	
08-08	HJW	Map Skills	Social Studies	worksheet, test	1xxx		x						use of maps
09-09	TJS	Latin America	Area Studies	test	1xxx	X	x	x	x	X	X		test taking strategies–task definition, synthesis
09-09	TJS	Northern Africa	Area Studies	test, report	x2xx		X	X	X	X	x		sources–web searching, note-taking
09-09	TJS	India	Area Studies	maps, product	xx3x		X	X	X	X	X	present, graphing software	computer software to create various kinds of maps
10-10	ALR	Industrial Revolution	US History	report	x2xx	X	X	X	x	X	X	WWW, elec res, word proc, present, e-mail	major reports–all Big6
10-10	ALR	Women's Suffrage	US Histroy	project	xx3x		x	X				WWW	
10-10	ALR	America Today	US History	project	xxx4	X						WWW, elec res, word proc	
10-10	WAJ	Constitution	US History	written and oral report	x2xx					X	X	present, word processing	Power Point
10-10	WAJ	Civil War	US History	test	xx3x	X				X	X		nature of test
10-10	AAR	Colonization of Western Hem.	US history	test	1xxx	X			x				extracting relevant information from the textbook and notes
10-10	AAR	Civil War	US History	report, project	xx3x		X	X	X				using primary and secondary resources
11-11	JAR	Between the Wars	World History	test, short written assignment, project	12xx					X			essay writing strategies
11-11	JAR	WWI	World History	test	1xxx	X				X			
11-11	JAR	WWII	World History	project;test	x2xx		X	x		X		WWW	Web-based information
11-11	JAR	Vietnam	World History	oral report	xx34		x	x	x	X	x	present, graphing software	PowerPoint
11-11	JAR	Cold War	World History	test	xx3x			X			X		
11-12	ALR	Stock Market	Economics	project	1234	X	X	X	X	x	X	WWW, elec res	full-year, competitive intelligence
11-12	ALR	Economic Institutions	Economics	report	xxx4	x	X	X	X	x	x	WWW, elec res, word proc, present, graphics, e-mail	
11-12	ALR	The New Information Economy	Economics	industry analysis and profile	xxx4				X	X	X	WWW, elec res, word proc, present, graphics, e-mail	
11-12	Petruso	Street Law	Legal Studies	project	xxx4		X			X			community resources and law libraries

Information. Jackson will teach the same topic but assess with a test. He will teach a lesson that reminds students of what they learned about test-taking in other grades and focus on the task definition aspects.

Mr. Ryan in grade 11 World History is a major Big6 "fan" and he plans to integrate Big6 instruction across five units. Again, as with Ms. Sullivan, he will focus on one or two of the Big6 within a given unit, but by the end of the year he will have covered all six stages in depth. Ryan (along with the technology teacher) also brings technology into the process—teaching Web searching in the World War II unit and using presentation and graphics software to create visuals for the Vietnam oral report.

The 12th grade teachers—Petruso and Valesky—teach senior elective courses. They are new to the Big6, but at a team meeting indicated that they were willing to give it a go. Petruso and the library media specialist are interested in introducing the students to resources in the community and special law libraries. Valesky will focus on comparing the value of all types of information resources.

Figure 4.3 focuses on grade 11, and indicates Big6 units throughout the year. The matrix also helps to compare across teachers—to determine possible areas for collaboration and to help avoid conflicting demands for resources.

For example, we see that the health teacher, Ms. Rausch (CER) teaches three major units with Big6 connections. Health is a one-half year course, so the units actually are repeated twice and eventually includes all students. Therefore, these are excellent units for Big6 instruction. Ms. Rausch teaches all of the Big6 with a particular emphasis on technology. One of her major concerns is that students learn to think critically about health information sources, so she focuses on Big6 #4—Use of Information—in all her units.

Mr. Carle (CJC), Mr. Wasik (RBW), Mrs. Bonzi (MAB) also plan to integrate the Big6 and technology into their subject area units for the first time. Mr. Carle wants students to dig out unique literacy criticism sources for their study of Salinger and Catcher in the Rye. Mr. Wasik will teach students how to use electronic spreadsheets to organize and present their laboratory results, Big6 #5—Synthesis. Mrs. Bonzi will have students use the WWW and other electronic resources to search for recipes and background information for her Spanish cooking unit, Big6 #2—Information Seeking Strategies and Big6 #3—Location & Access.

Figure 4.3 is also useful for highlighting common units and time frames. We see that Carle, Wasik, Ryan, and Robinson are all teaching the Big6 in the third marking period to 11th and 12th grade students. Some students may be in two or all three classes. And, if the students are in health as well, they may receive Big6 instruction from Rausch as well! This is clearly too much, so the teachers may wish to compare notes so they minimize duplication.

Planning and Plans on the School Level

It is also important to plan for systematic Big6 Skills instruction at the school level. The goal is to ensure that students have a range of Big6 instructional experiences across grade levels and subjects. These experiences should

The Big6

GR	TCHR	UNIT	SUBJECT	ASSIGNMENT	M_PER	1	2	3	4	5	6	TECHNOLOGY	COMMENTS
09-12	NOU	Career	Drama	report, project	xx3x	X	X	X		X		WWW, elec res	
09-12	CER	Diet & Nutrition	Health	posters	1x3x	X	X	X	X	X	X	WWW, *PowerPoint*	all students take health; repeats 2x year, stress critical evaluation of info
09-12	CER	Tobacco & Smoking	Health	test	1x3x	X			X	X	X		cooperative teacher, test-taking strategies & the Big6
09-12	CER	Drugs	Health	product	x2x4	X	X	X	X	X	X	WWW, elec res, word proc, present	
11-11	JAR	Between the Wars	SS—World History	test, short written assignment	12xx					X			essay writing strategies
11-11	JAR	WWI	SS—World History	test	1xxx	X							
11-11	JAR	WWII	SS—World History	project, test	x2xx		X	X	x	X		WWW	Web-based information
11-11	JAR	Vietnam	SS—World History	oral report	xx34		x	x	X	X	x	present, graphing software	*PowerPoint*
11-11	JAR	Cold War	SS—World History	test	xx3x						X		
11-12	CJC	*Catcher in the Rye*	English	report	xx3x		X	X					literacy criticism resources
11-12	RBW	Light Lab	Sci Physics	lab report, test	xx3x					X		spreadsheets	
11-12	MAB	Spanish Cooking	Spanish 4	product	xxx4		X	X				WWW, elec res, word proc	
11-12	ALR	Stock Market	SS—Economics	project	1234	X	X	X	X	X	X	WWW, elec res	full-year, competitive intelligence
11-12	ALR	Economic Institutions	SS—Economics	report	xx3x		X	x	x	X	X	WWW, elec res, word proc	major project–Big6 focus printed or Web-based
11-12	ALR	The New Information Economy	SS—Economics	industry analysis and profile	xxx4	x	X	X	X	x	x	WWW, elec res, word proc, present, graphics, e-mail	

GR	TCHR	UNIT	SUBJECT	ASSIGNMENT	M_PER	The Big6						TECHNOLOGY	COMMENTS
						1	2	3	4	5	6		
07-07	TMJ	Weather	Sci	test	xx3x	x						WWW, elec res, word proc, present, e-mail	lots of technology
07-07	TCH	Recycling	Social Studies	product	x23x	x	x	x	x		x		
08-08	RTD	Mysteries	English	video	1xxx	x				x		WWW, elec res, word proc, present, e-mail	build on grade 7, technology
08-08	TMJ	Noise	Sci, General	written report	x2xx	x	x	x	x	x	x		
08-08	CGR	Rainforest	Social Studies	test, short written	1xxx			x	x			WWW, word proc	
08-08	HJW	Map Skills	Social Studies	worksheet, test	1xxx		x		x				use of maps
09-09	TJS	Latin America	Area Studies	test	1xxx	x	x	x	x	x	x		test taking strategies–task definition, synthesis
09-09	TJS	Northern Africa	Area Studies	test, report	x2xx		x	x	x	x	x	WWW, elec res	sources–web searching, note-taking
09-09	TJS	India	Area Studies	maps, product	xx3x					x	x	present, graphing software	computer software to create various kinds of maps
09-12	NOU	Career	Drama	report, project	xx3x	x	x	x				WWW, elec res	
09-12	CER	Diet & Nutrition	Health	posters	1x3x	x	x	x	x	x	x	WWW, *PowerPoint*	all students take health; repeats 2x year, stress critical evaluation of info
09-12	CER	Tabacco & Smoking	Health	test	1x3x	x			x	x	x		cooperative teacher, test-taking strategies & the Big6
09-12	CER	Drugs	Health	product	x2x4x	x	x	x	x	x	x	WWW, elec res, word proc, present	
10-10	MBE	Web authoring	Library	product (Web page)	x2xx		x		x	x		*Front Page*, HTML, scanner	
10-10	BAB	Probability	Math	homework	xx3x			x	x			spreadsheets	
10-10	CAL	Anatomy	Sci, Biology	oral presentation	1xxx		x	x	x	x		WWW, *PowerPoint*	major emphasis on *PowerPoint* skills organizing info
10-10	CAL	Circulatory System	Sci, Biology	worksheets	x2xx	x			x				compile worksheets, targeted analysis
10-10	CAL	Digestive System	Sci, Biology	group presentations	xx3x	x	x	x	x	x	x	WWW, *PowerPoint*	review Big6

Figure 4.4 continued

GR	TCHR	UNIT	SUBJECT	ASSIGNMENT	M_PER	1	2	3	4	5	6	TECHNOLOGY	COMMENTS
10-10	AAR	Colonization of Western Hemisphere	US History	test	1xxx	X							extracting relevant information from the textbooks and notes
10-10	ALR	Industrial Revolution	US History	report	x2xx	X	X	X	X	X	X	WWW, elec res, word proc, present, e-mail	major reports–all Big6
10-10	WAJ	Constitution	US History	written and oral report	x2xx					X	X	present, word processing	PowerPoint
10-10	ALR	Women's Suffrage	US History	project	xx3x		X	X				WWW	
10-10	WAJ	Civil War	US History	test	xx3x	X							nature of test
10-10	AAR	Civil War	US History	report, project	xx3x		X	X	X				using primary and secondary sources
10-10	ALR	America Today	US History	project	xxx4	X				X		WWW, elec res, Word proc	
11-11	JAR	Between the Wars	World History	test, short written assignment, project	12xx					X			essay writing strategies
11-11	JAR	WWI	World History	test	1xxx	X				X			
11-11	JAR	WWII	World History	project, test	x2xx		x	x	x	x		WWW	Web-based information
11-11	JAR	Vietnam	World History	oral report	xx34		x	x	x	x	x	present, graphing software	PowerPoint
11-11	JAR	Cold War	World History	test	xx3x						x		
11-12	ALR	Stock Market	Economics	project	1234	X	X	X	X	X	X	WWW, elec res	full-year, competitive intelligence
11-12	ALR	Economic Institutions	Economics	report	xx3x	x	x	x	x	x	x	WWW, elec res, word proc	major project–Big6 focus; printed or Web-based
11-12	ALR	The New Information Economy	Economics	industry analysis and profile	xxx4	x	x	x	x	x	x	WWW, elec res, word proc, present, graphics, e-mail	
11-12	CJC	Catcher in the Rye	English	report	xx3x		x	x					literacy criticism resources
11-12	Petruso	Street Law	Legal Studies	project	xxx4		x			x			community resources and law libraries
11-12	RBW	Light Lab	Sci, Physics	lab report, test	xx3x					x		spreadsheets	
11-12	MAB	Spanish Cooking	Spanish 4	product	xxx4		x	x				WWW, elec res, word proc	
12-12	LSZ	Senior Research Paper	English	term paper	xxx4	x	x	x	x	x	x	tools, info	
13-13	SEC	Printed Formats: Magazines	Media Studies	short written assignment, test	1xxx	x			X	X		WWW, elec res, word proc	

build upon each other so that by the end of their K-12 education, each student has had ample opportunities to develop competencies in specific technology and information skills within the overall Big6 context.

School-wide Big6 planning requires cooperation among classroom teachers, library media specialists, technology teachers, and administrators. From experience, we find that active, engaged library media specialists are in an ideal position to coordinate the school-wide Big6 Skills effort. First, information skills instruction is a major function of library media programs. In addition, library media specialists are involved with instruction across the curriculum. They are responsible for providing resources and services to all grades and subjects and generally have an excellent overview of the existing school curriculum. Therefore, we recommend, when possible, that library media specialists coordinate Big6 planning with technology teachers, classroom teachers, administrators, and support staff.

Figure 4.4 is a partially completed Big6 by Unit Matrix for a secondary school covering grades 7–12. At this point, the matrix only includes some of the units slated for integrated Big6 instruction. The library media specialist is compiling this plan, and has worked on documenting integrated units across the grade levels and subject areas. The units that involve extensive Big6 instruction with three or more planned Big6 lessons are:

- 7th grade – recycling – social studies
- 8th grade – noise – science
- 9th grade – Latin America – social studies
- 9th grade – Northern Africa – social studies
- 9th – 12th grade – diet and nutrition – health
- 9th – 12th grade – tobacco and smoking – health
- 10th grade – anatomy – science
- 10th grade – digestive system – science
- 10th grade – industrial revolution – social studies
- 10th grade – Civil War – social studies (Rossini, not Jackson)
- 11th-12th grade – stock market – social studies
- 11th-12th grade – economic institutions – social studies
- 11th-12th grade – the new economy – social studies.

These extensive units are supplemented by Big6 instruction in other classes as well. However, there is still room for expansion of the integrated information and technology skills instructional program. Expanded collaboration among teachers can be coordinated by the library media specialist and technology teachers. The goal is to expand this plan to ensure that all students have formal opportunities to learn Big6 and technology skills. The matrix is a useful planning tool for this, and later it becomes the documentation for the implemented program.

Summary

Systematic planning for integrated Big6 Skills instruction is essential if we are to make a difference in our classrooms and schools. If we truly believe that information and technology skills are essential for student success, then we must make sure that students have frequent opportunities to learn and practice these skills.

It's not enough to work with students one-on-one or to offer an isolated lesson in note taking or Web search engines. Students need lessons in each of the Big6 Skills, delivered in the context of the real, subject area assignments. Accomplishing comprehensive, integrated Big6 instruction requires classroom teachers, library media specialists, technology teachers, and administrators to make a concerted and systematic effort to plan and document their efforts.

Figure 4.5 is a blank Big6 Skills by Unit Matrix to help you get started.

Reflections

Figure 4.5: *Blank Big6™ Skills by Unit Matrix: Secondary School*

The Big6™

GR	TCHR	UNIT	SUBJECT	ASSIGNMENT	M_PER	1	2	3	4	5	6	TECHNOLOGY	COMMENTS

CHAPTER 5

Assessment of Information & Technology Skills

Introduction

While not always the most enjoyable part of learning and teaching, assessment is nevertheless essential to help students attain higher levels of achievement. This is particularly important in relation to the Big6, as we believe that competence in information problem-solving is a key to success in every curriculum area.

By assessing students' skills in each of the Big6, we can pinpoint strengths and weaknesses and target areas for further development. We can also assess how well students are able to apply the Big6 process to a range of tasks and offer additional instruction as necessary.

Effective assessment should communicate teacher expectations, provide motivation, and also enable students to assess themselves. To do so, educators should consider the following:

- The specific content-learning goals
- Related Big6 Skills
- Criteria for assessment, and
- Evidence to examine to determine student performance.

Assessment that focuses on instructional objectives and is based on established criteria helps teachers to appropriately modify and target instruction. Assessment can also help educators determine whether students are eligible for advanced instruction or if students need special, individualized assistance.

Assessment can be defined as making judgments based on a predetermined set of criteria. From a Big6 perspective, two broad criteria for assessment are effectiveness and efficiency.

Effectiveness and Efficiency

Two key criteria of assessment are part of stage #6—Evaluation—in the Big6 process:

> **6.1 Effectiveness of the product.**
> **6.2 Efficiency of the process.**

Students learn to assess the results of their efforts by analyzing the effectiveness of their product and their efficient use of the Big6 process to complete various tasks and create various products.

Even young children can learn to judge whether they are effective, (having done a good job or worthy of a good grade) or efficient (not wasting time and effort). As students get older, they can assume more and more responsibility for their own achievement and assessment of that achievement.

In relation to effectiveness, students can learn to judge their own products. Students can diagnose the result of their effort when they learn to do such things as the following:

- Compare the requirements to the results
- Check the appropriateness and accuracy of the information they use
- Judge how well their solution is organized
- Rate the quality of their final product or performance compared to their potential (i.e., Did I do the best that I could?)
- Judge the quality of their product to a predefined standard.

These, of course, are rather sophisticated actions. Less sophisticated learners can still ask themselves such questions as:

- Is my project good; how do I know?
- Am I proud of my project?

Assessing efficiency requires students to evaluate the nature, tendencies, and preferences of their personal information problem-solving process. This is sometimes referred to as "meta-cognition"—recognizing how we learn, process information, and solve problems. With the Big6, we can help students learn how to assess the efficiency of the process they use to reach decisions and solutions. Some assessment techniques to facilitate this include the following:

- Keeping and evaluating a log of activities
- Reflecting back on the sequence of events and judging effort and time involved

- Reviewing and analyzing the areas of frustration and barriers they encountered
- Rating their abilities to perform specific information problem-solving actions. (i.e., locating, note-taking, skimming, scanning, prioritizing).

Simply stated, students can begin by asking themselves the following:

- Am I pleased with my effort?
- What was easy and what was difficult?
- How could I do better next time?

These are the types of questions that teachers can build into activities and assignments.

Forms and Context for Assessment

There are two broad forms of assessment—summative and formative. Summative is after-the-fact assessment, designed to determine the degree of student learning after they have completed a lesson, unit, or other instructional event. Assessing students' performance on the overall information problem-solving process through a project, report, or assignment, for example, is summative assessment. Formative assessment involves providing feedback so that adjustments can be made before students turn in their work. Formative assessment of information and technology skills might involve assessing students' work at each stage of the Big6.

Classroom teachers, library media specialists and other educators can either provide feedback at each step of the information problem-solving process; when the assignment, project, or product is completed; or both.

Throughout this book, we emphasize that the Big6 Skills are best learned in the context of real curriculum needs. School curriculum is rich and detailed at all grade levels, and Big6 Skills instruction can easily be integrated with a range of subjects and topics. Assessment of Big6 Skills is similarly best conducted within real curriculum contexts. That means finding ways to determine students' abilities in the overall process and individual Big6 Skills as they complete various homework assignments, projects, reports, products, and tests.

Most often, the focus of assessment is on evaluating how well students are doing with just the classroom content. Content learning is clearly of major importance. But, we must also be concerned with process skills as embodied by the Big6. How effective and efficient are students overall and in the specific skills necessary to solve information problems?

Effective assessment speaks to many audiences:

- To students—to let them know how they are doing and how they can improve
- To teachers—to help them determine whether students are learning the content and skills

- To parents—to keep them informed about the level of success of their children and how they might help them.

Assessment should measure performance in a manner that is easily understood by all audiences. In addition, good assessment strategies do the following:

- Reflect the objectives of the lesson or unit
- Measure the behavior described by the objective
- Make certain that students fully understand all assessment criteria
- Provide constructive feedback on strengths and weaknesses.

Ways of Assessing

Assessing the Big6 Skills in context includes the following key elements:

- Evidence to examine to determine student performance
- The specific content-learning goals
- Related Big6 Skills
- Criteria for judging
- A rating scale for judging, and
- The judgments themselves.

Each element is essential to successful assessment and is explained in more detail below.

Evidence

As stated, assessment of Big6 Skills should take place within the context of real curriculum needs. In practice, that means looking carefully at assignments. For a given curriculum unit, teachers select one or more assignments to emphasize the importance of content and skills, to motivate students and to evaluate student performance. In most instances, assignments will comprise the "evidence" of assessing Big6 learning. Other options include observing student performance, talking to students during or after working on an assignment, or having students engage in self-assessment activities. Typical assignments include the following:

- Homework other than worksheets
- Worksheets
- Exercises
- Reports or research papers
- Projects
- Quizzes or tests.

Content Learning Goals

Content learning goals include the skills and topics of the subject area curriculum. These can be established by individual classroom teachers or designated by a standard curriculum at the school, district, region, or state level.

Big6™ Learning Goals

It is not necessary or desirable to assess all the Big6 in every assignment. In fact, it can become tedious to do so. Therefore, we encourage educators to focus assessment on the Big6 Skills that were (1) taught, or (2) particularly important to the learning and assignment.

Criteria for Judging

Assessment criteria should be clearly defined statements of intended learner outcomes. Criteria should describe competence levels and should be designed to measure students' achievement toward instructional goals. For the Big6 Skills, criteria should relate to students' abilities in applying the Big6 to the content learning goals. To assist teachers, sample criteria statements for each stage of the Big6 are provided in Figure 5.1.

A Rating Scale for Judging

Rating scales are used as an indication of a student's learning state on criteria at a given point in time. The scale can be a simple numbered order, labels, or even symbols:

Low			High
1	2	3	4
Needs work	Okay	Well done	Super
Oops! See me, please.	You did 3/5 requirements far!	One more draft, please.	Bravo!

The less able the students, the more we suggest avoiding any numerical scales. The main point is that teachers and students need to have a simple way to express the learning state.

The Judgments Themselves

To make developing and implementing judgments easier, we created Big6 Scoring Guides. These guides combine the various elements of assessment in a straightforward form. In the next section, we give specific examples of how to use a scoring guide.

Figure 5.1: *Sample Criteria Statements for the Big6™*

Task Definition
The student demonstrates the ability to:
- Determine the information problem to be solved
- Clearly define the task
- Identify the important elements of the task
- Show complete understanding of the task and its parts
- Pick out keywords embedded in a question
- Ask good questions
- Understand and follow printed and/or oral directions.

Information Seeking Strategies
The student demonstrates the ability to:
- Develop an approach to seeking a variety of materials
- Determine which information sources are most/least important
- Determine which information sources are most/least appropriate
- Demonstrate knowledge of relevant sources
- Recognize that information can be gained from many sources including investigation and observation
- Understand the value of human resources
- Use appropriate criteria for selecting sources, including readability, scope, authority, currency, usefulness, and format.

Location & Access
The student demonstrates the ability to:
- Gather resources independently
- Ask questions to obtain information
- Determine what sources are available
- Access appropriate information systems, including: online databases, catalog-master list, electronic multimedia.

Use of Information
The student demonstrates the ability to:
- Paraphrase the main idea accurately from written, visual and/or oral source material
- Summarize the main idea from written, visual and/or oral source material
- Distinguish facts from opinions
- Gather information carefully (read, listen, and/or view)
- Cite sources accurately.

Synthesis
The student demonstrates the ability to:
- Prepare an accurate bibliography of all resources (Internet and other resources)
- Organize information
- Present information
- Use a standard bibliographic format
- Prepare charts, graphs, outlines, etc.
- Compare and contrast points of view from several sources
- Summarize and retell information from multiple sources
- Design products to communicate content.

Evaluation
The student demonstrates the ability to:
- Assess projects for strengths and weaknesses
- Provide recommendations for improving the information problem-solving result
- Judge solutions and decisions
- Assess the completeness of the response to the assigned task
- Review and critique the steps used in solving an information problem.

Big6™ Scoring Guides

In addition to pulling together all the requisite elements of assessment, Big6 Scoring Guides are designed to communicate teachers' expectations for students' work in ways that students can understand and use. Big6 Scoring Guides focus on the information problem-solving process as well as the final result. Therefore, guides are useful both during and after working on assignments—for both formative and summative assessment.

As stated above, formative assessment involves diagnosing students' performance during learning so that adjustments can be made before students turn in their work. Adjustments may include the following:

- Redirecting planned instruction to focus on areas where students are having trouble
- Providing special learning activities not previously planned
- Helping students to apply relevant technology tools
- Redefining the problem or returning to a previous Big6 stage
- Offering one-on-one tutoring
- Brainstorming alternative approaches.

These types of adjustments are prescriptions for improving learning. Of course, Big6 Scoring Guides can also be used to assess final products—summative assessment. Many teachers find that post-assignment debriefings—built around Big6 Scoring Guides—are effective ways to involve students in the assessment process.

It's relatively easy to create a Big6 Scoring Guide:

1. Define the curriculum objectives within a Big6 context.
2. Determine which Big6 Skills are important (the focus) for the particular assignment.
3. Develop criteria across a scale (i.e., from "highly competent" to "not yet acceptable"). There may be more than one aspect to each criterion. Consider which aspects are essential.
4. Determine what evidence will be examined to determine student performance for each Big6 Skill.
5. Conduct the assessment.
6. Share the assessment with students.
7. Determine and document the level of achievement.
8. Revise as necessary.

For example, assume that completing the worksheet in figure 5.2 is the task for students in ninth-grade biology studying "muscular activity." Figure 5.3 is the Big6 Scoring Guide designed to assess students' performance. This guide is designed to include multiple assessments—by student (S), teacher

(T), or library media specialist (L). This allows students and teachers to quickly identify gaps in their views of perceived performance. Focusing on gaps can lead to clarification of misunderstandings and can highlight the need for further instruction.

The column labeled "Evidence" is used to indicate the products or techniques to be used to assess specific skills. Examples of evidence include written, visual, or oral products, assignments, homework, projects, tests, observation, or even self-reflection. This is an essential piece of the Scoring Guide since it identifies the specific context for assessing student performance.

The last column, "Focus," relates to the relative importance of each skill being evaluated. It is not necessary or desirable to assess all Big6 Skills equally in every learning situation. The assigned focus should be based on the goals and objectives of the unit in terms of Big6 skill development and content learning. For example, in the muscle example, a percentage of emphasis is assigned to each of the Big6. Location & Access is not a skill emphasized in this situation while the focus is on Task Definition and Synthesis.

Self-Assessment

Continuous self-assessment is an integral part of the Big6. When students engage in Big6 #6—Evaluation-activities, they are conducting self-assessment. In addition to having students reflect on their own abilities, self-assessment fosters independence and responsibility in students. Through self-assessment, students learn to translate expectations into action, build on their accomplishments, and work on weaknesses. And yet, it is important to remember that students are better able to assess their work when they have a scoring system. This system may resemble a teacher's scoring guide. It can be as simple as a checklist of the required elements for the assignment. It can be more complicated, asking students to grade themselves and provide a rationale. As teachers, you need to consider your own and your students' needs for appropriate assessment tools.

Teachers can reinforce self-assessment by involving students in developing criteria, grading schemes, and Big6 Scoring Guides. Teachers can also help students to generalize from "schoolwork assessment" (e.g. on projects, tests, assignments) to success in areas of personal interest (e.g. sports, art, music, hobbies), and ultimately at work (e.g. job satisfaction, salary, making a contribution).

It is difficult, if not impossible, for students to do their best if they don't know how to recognize it when they see it. All too often, students are left to guess at such things as whether they are finished with an assignment or whether they have done a good job on an assignment. Students should be able to compare their efforts with their teachers' expectations and with established standards. When necessary, students need to revise or redirect their effort. And, self-assessment may result in students realizing that they need to learn new skills.

Figure 5.2: *Ninth Grade Science Laboratory Experiment: Muscular Action Worksheet*

Ninth Grade Science Laboratory Experiment:
Muscular Action Worksheet

Your task is to design a controlled experiment to test the hypothesis below. Your experiment should be designed so that it can be conducted in a 15 to 20 minute period.

Hypothesis:

When there is an increase in muscular activity, there is a corresponding increase in the energy used by muscles. This energy increase causes heat as well as a corresponding increase in oxygen consumption.

Material:

Procedure:

Result: (tabulate data and represent in an appropriate graph)

Conclusion:

Questions:
- What variable(s) did you test?
- What are the constants?
- What was the experimental control?
- Evaluation/Scoring Guide

Big6™ Scoring Guide for Secondary Science Muscular Action Laboratory Experiment

Big6™ Skills	Highly Competent 10 points	Competent 8 points	Adequate 7 points	Not Yet Acceptable 5 points	Evidence	Focus
Eisenberg/Berkowitz © 1997			Criteria			
1. Task Definition 1.1 Define the problem. 1.2 Identify the information needed. S T L	Experiment meets 15-20 minute requirements. Procedure tested: oxygen consumption & levels of heat.	Experiment limited to 15-20 minute requirements. Procedure tested: oxygen consumption or level of heat, but not both.	Experiment did not meet time requirement. Procedure tested: oxygen consumption or level of heat, but not both.	Experiment did not meet time requirement. Procedure did not test for either; oxygen consumption or levels of heat.	Experiment	20%
2. Information Seeking Strategies 2.1 Determine all possible sources. 2.2 Select the best sources. S T L	Procedure can be repeated exactly and produce the same results. Procedure tests the hypothesis.	Procedure tested the hypothesis, but is not easily followed.	Procedure tested the hypothesis, but is not easily followed, and does not give the same results.	Procedure does not test the hypothesis. Procedure cannot be repeated at all.	Procedure	40%
3. Location & Access 3.1 Locate sources. 3.2 Find information within sources. S T L						
4. Use of Information 4.1 Engage (e.g., read hear, view, and touch). 4.2 Extract relevant information. S T L	Complete and accurate data tables. Complete and appropriate graphs.	Accurate data tables. Appropriate but incomplete graphs.	Incomplete data tables. Incomplete and inaccurate graphs.	No data tables. No graphs.	Results	10%
5. Synthesis 5.1 Organize information from multiple sources. 5.2 Present the result. S T L	Appropriate conclusion. Answers all questions completely.	Appropriate conclusion. Answers all questions poorly.	Conclusion attempted, but inappropriate. Questions poorly answered and/or only some questions answered.	No Conclusion. No questions answered.	Conclusion Question	20%
6. Evaluation 6.1 Judge the result. 6.2 Judge the process. S T L	Scoring Guide thoughtfully completed.			Scoring Guide not completed.	Scoring Guide	10%

We believe it is crucial to help students to learn to do the following:

- Assess their own information problem-solving styles
- Value and recognize quality work
- Reflect on the ways they go about tackling assignments and tasks
- Determine how they can improve, and
- Learn how to establish criteria to evaluate their results.

Students don't often take the initiative to self-assess because they haven't been encouraged to do so, may not see the value in self-assessment, or may not know how. That's where the Big6 approach comes in. The Big6 reminds us that evaluation is essential to the process. Teachers must prepare students to learn self-assessment in the context of curriculum, personal, or work situations.

Feelings are an important part of self-assessment. Students may lack confidence and pride in their work because they don't really know if they have done a good job. Sometimes, feelings of confidence and pride are replaced with frustration and disappointment when students get their assignment back with a poor grade when they expected to do well. Self-assessment helps students and teachers to apply the same evaluation criteria to the students' work. Students learn to look at their work through their teachers' eyes. In this way, students can build on strengths and identify areas for improvement. Students gain insight into specific areas to improve their performance. This can boost confidence, pride, and encourage a higher level of academic success.

We often assume that students are able to rate the quality of their products or the effectiveness of their information problem-solving approach, but of course, this is not always the case. Self-assessment skills should not be assumed–they should be part of the instructional program. Students need to learn, recognize, and apply the standards of excellence. Again, it's helping students to learn to view their own work in the way teachers view students' work.

Summary

Assessment is an important part of learning and essential to the learning of Big6 Skills. As with Big6 Skills instruction, Big6 assessment should be integrated with classroom curriculum. Existing assignments provide ample opportunities to assess individual Big6 Skills as well as overall information problem-solving abilities. There are requisite elements to assessment which are pulled together in the Big6 Scoring Guides. We include a blank scoring guide (Figure 5.4) to help you get started.

This blank guide is designed to include multiple assessments—by student (S), teacher (T), or library media specialist (L). This allows students and teachers to quickly identify gaps in their views of perceived performance. Focusing on gaps can lead to clarification of misunderstandings and can highlight the need for further instruction.

The column labeled "Evidence" is used to indicate the products or techniques to be used to assess specific skills. Examples of evidence include written, visual, or oral products, assignments, homework, projects, tests, observation, or even self-reflection. This is an essential piece of the Scoring Guide since it identifies the specific context for assessing student performance.

The last column, "Focus," relates to the relative importance of each skill being evaluated. It is not necessary or desirable to assess all Big6 Skills equally in every learning situation. The assigned focus should be based on the goals and objectives of the unit in terms of Big6 Skill development and content learning.

Figure 5.4: *Blank Big6™ Scoring Guide*

Big6™ Assessment Scoring Guide

Criteria →

Big6™ Skills	Highly Competent 10 points	Competent 8 points	Adequate 7 points	Not Yet Acceptable 5 points	Evidence	Focus
Eisenberg/Berkowitz © 1997						
1. Task Definition 1.1 Define the problem. 1.2 identify the information needed.	S T L	S T L	S T L			
2. Information Seeking Strategies 2.1 Determine all possible sources. 2.2 Select the best sources.	S T L	S T L	S T L			
3. Location & Access 3.1 Locate sources. 3.2 Find information within sources.	S T L	S T L	S T L			
4. Use of Information 4.1 Engage (e.g., read hear, view, and touch). 4.2 Extract relevant information.	S T L	S T L	S T L			
5. Synthesis 5.1 Organize information from multiple sources. 5.2 Present the result.	S T L	S T L	S T L			
6. Evaluation 6.1 Judge the result. 6.2 Judge the process.	S T L	S T L	S T L			

Reflections

PART II

The Big6™ in Action

Introduction

The first section of this book sets out the theoretical framework of the Big6, and, in general terms, describes how it is applied in various contexts. This is certainly valuable, but teachers also want to see how the Big6 works in a real classroom situation. That's the purpose of Part II: to present the Big6 in action through further explanations, sample integrated lesson plans, and Big6 activities.

    Part II is organized around each component of Big6. We will guide you with teaching information problem-solving ("TIPS") explanations applicable to each Big6 Skill, and answer commonly asked questions. Perhaps the most valuable feature of this section are the sample lesson plans. They encompass a variety of grades and subject matter. As part of an integrated curriculum, they demonstrate how the various aspects of the Big6 can be taught together or as separate skills. These lessons are for demonstration purposes only. You will want to extract ideas from them, explore other approaches and possibilities, and adapt the content to your program's needs. We cannot overemphasize these points—the sample lessons and activities should be adapted to your local situation and needs.

We encourage you to use this section of the book as an "idea generator." As you work to develop your students' information problem-solving skills, the first section will provide you with direction concerning why you do what you do. And, the second section will help you think of effective ways to do what you do. Think of it as a Big6 challenge for you personally. That is, approach each lesson's goals and objectives as your own information problem to solve. In designing your instructional units and lessons you need to define the task, identify a range of sources that will help you create an appropriate lesson, find the right set of sources, use the information within the sources, actually create the lesson, and evaluate whether your students actually learned the skills you intended your lesson to teach.

So use the Big6 as your guide to developing curriculum and instruction. After all, as educators we are best able to teach those skills we mastered by practice and implementation ourselves.

Reflections

CHAPTER 6

Big6™ #1: Task Definition

Task Definition is the first stage in the Big6 process. Task Definition has two components:

1.1 Define the problem.
1.2 Identify the information needed.

Task Definition is a key to success in homework, assignments, and tests, yet it is often ignored or overlooked in terms of specific, formal instruction. Teachers don't intentionally give vague or confusing assignments, but students often have trouble understanding what's expected of them. In our *Helping With Homework* (1996) book, we describe a situation where I spoke to a class about a test they were supposed to have on the following Monday. Only about one-quarter of the class really knew what was going to be on the test, the type of test they would be taking, and what material they should study. Yes, the teacher had gone over the directions, but the students hadn't really "heard" it. Perhaps they were daydreaming, had something else on their minds, or truly didn't understand the directions.

Big6 TIPS: Task Definition
The solution to this problem is not for the teacher to go over the assignment again, but to help the students assume responsibility for their own tasks. We want to move the focus of responsibility for the assignment from

the teacher to the students. For example, we encourage students to do "brain surgery" on their teachers. "Get inside your teachers' heads—quiz the teachers on expectations, criteria for assessment, and key elements. Don't let the teacher move on to something else until you fully understand all aspects of the assignment."

One tip to encourage student responsibility is to purposely give assignments without much explanation. "You are to create travel brochures on countries." That's all the direction you need to give. This method forces the students to find out the details and can lead to a stimulating exchange on options, key aspects, and grading.

Another goal for Task Definition instruction is transferability—to have students apply their skills and knowledge beyond school situations. A hallmark of the Big6 is its broad applicability. While most library skills instruction centers on reports or projects, we encourage working on Task Definition with a wide range of tasks and problems.

All students have curriculum-based information problems to solve, for example:

- A kindergarten group learning about signs of spring
- A 3rd grade class making charts on food groups
- 6th graders studying why certain animal species are endangered
- 12th grade language arts students studying modern world authors
- A university economics class analyzing the impact of the Internet on global markets.

But we need to help students recognize that the Big6 also applies to problems and tasks they face every day, for example:

- Deciding what television show to watch
- Preparing for a basketball game
- Picking out a birthday present for a friend.

So, in addition to applying the Big6 to specific curriculum situations, teachers and library media specialists can work together to develop lessons that develop skills related to everyday situations. Lessons built around these and other personal information tasks have proved extremely motivating and useful in helping students recognize how the Big6 can be applied to lots of different situations.

For example, we like to organize students in triads—where students assume one of three roles—a talker who explains a problem, a listener/questioner who probes for detail, and a recorder who writes it all down. Later the students switch roles so that each one has a chance to do all three. Finally, the students report back on the problem they recorded (not on their own)—orally to the whole class, in writing to the teacher, or both.

Another tip is to have students keep a "Task Definition Log" for a week or so. Work with the students to develop (1) the criteria for what makes a task or problem, (2) what data they will record, and (3) a chart for recording the data.

The logs can be discussed each day as well as summarized in final presentations that delve into the nature of tasks and problems, and how information, the Big6 Skills, and technology relate to them.

All of the above tips focus on the "defining the problem" component of Task Definition. In the Big6 model, Task Definition also includes "identifying the information" requirements of the problem. Here, we want students to consider various aspects of the information they will need to solve the task/problem—before they begin thinking about specific resources. For example, we want students to reflect on things like:

- The type of information (facts, opinions; primary or secondary)
- The amount of information (single source, a few resources, comprehensive)
- The format of information (text, graphics, audio, video).

These considerations are especially important today since technology is providing many different options for packaging information. Tips to help students learn to focus on information requirements include lessons where they brainstorm options related to their curriculum tasks and assignments. We've also found it useful to develop a checklist where students can indicate the types, amounts, and formats of information they are seeking.

With a solid idea of their information requirements, students are ready to move on and determine and select possible resources—Big6 #2.

The Big6 Card

The Big6™ Skills Approach to Information Problem-Solving

1. Task Definition
1.1 Define the problem
1.2 Identify the information needed

2. Information Seeking Strategies
2.1 Determine all possible sources
2.2 Select the best sources

3. Location & Access
3.1 Locate sources
3.2 Find information within sources

4. Use of Information
4.1 Engage (e.g., read, hear, view)
4.2 Extract relevant information

5. Synthesis
5.1 Organize info from multiple sources
5.2 Present the result

6. Evaluation
6.1 Judge the result (effectiveness)
6.2 Judge the process (efficiency)

© Eisenberg and Berkowitz, 1987

Title: *Creating a Thesis*

Author: Kathleen L. Spitzer

Related Big6 Skills: Big 6 #1—Task Definition

Purpose: Students will examine their preliminary research to create a thesis statement.

Learning Contexts: This lesson is appropriate for secondary or higher education students who must develop and support a thesis statement.

Discussion: There are times when students must develop a thesis statement before they do any research on their topic. When one such student was asked what his thesis statement would be, he replied, "something about soccer." When told that he would need to further define what aspect of soccer he would investigate, he looked confused and asked, "what is a thesis statement?" The student was given some examples of thesis statements and was asked to recall what he knew about soccer. Would his topic fit into any of the categories? He was able to narrow his focus to: Pele has been the most influential player in soccer.

The thesis statement tip sheet provides students with helpful examples. Individual conferencing is also very productive. The library media specialist and teacher can ask each student what their thesis statement is and how they plan to support it. Students can then be redirected from poor choices, and additional ideas for research can be discussed.

Item: Developing a Thesis Statement handout

After students have a chance to research their topic, distribute the "developing a thesis statement" sheets. Students can reflect on their research and compare it to the sample thesis statements. They should write a thesis statement for their topic and discuss it with their teacher or the library media specialist.

Sample in Context: The culminating project for the senior English class is to write a ten (10) page paper that will support or disprove a thesis statement. Students must use in-text citations and provide a works cited page in MLA format.

Many students have difficulty identifying how their topic of interest can become a thesis statement. The thesis activity provides students with examples and with individual counseling to help coach them in a feasible direction.

Evaluate your thesis in terms of your research:

Is your thesis statement too broad?

If if is, narrow it.

Is your thesis statement too narrow?

If it is, broaden it.

Can your thesis statement be proven using your research?

If not, change your thesis statement to one that you can prove using your research.

Developing a Thesis Statement

After some preliminary research on your topic, develop a thesis that can be "proven" by your paper. Here are some examples:

Methods	Sample thesis statement
Chronologies: 1910 1920 1930 Event A Event B	The rise of the Third Reich took place over a period of years.
Procedures: 1 2 3 4	There are 17 steps that occur before a bill can become a law.
Cause and Effect: If A Then B	Acid rain has contributed to the death of many lakes and trees in the Adirondacks.
Problems:	Problems of religious intolerance forced the Pilgrims to come to the New World.
Solutions:	The elimination of aerosol sprays will help reduce ozone depletion.
Comparisons:	President Bush was a more effective leader than President Carter.
Similarities: B A	The political climates of both Italy and Germany prior to World War II were similar.
Differences:	Birth and death rates differ greatly among first world and third world countries.
Relationships: A B	It is evident that Poe's life influenced his work.
Analyses:	There were two major causes of the Gulf War.
Literary Themes:	Many of Shakespeare's sonnets feature romantic themes.
Pros:	Bush's decisive handling of the Gulf War boosted his position with Congress.
Cons:	Many government officials are opposed to limiting pollutants stating that to do so would be detrimental to the economy.
Categories: A B C	There are five major food groups.
Spacial:	The effects of acid rain may be felt all over the world.

Title: *Defining a Science Project Topic*

Author: Robert Darrow

Related Big6 Skills: Big6 #1—Task Definition

Purpose: This lesson will help students define a science fair project research topic.

Learning Contexts: Grades 5-12

Discussion: Science classes come into the library media center to find background research for their science projects. Most students have a "research question" but they don't know their research topic. Science teachers often give students a list of possible research questions such as: "How does light effect plant growth?" In this example students are not sure whether to look for information about light, or plant, or growth, or plant growth. To begin research, students need to define their topic.

To measure student success on Task Definition of a science research topic, a verbal response by each student indicates if he or she has the correct keyword for finding information.

Students need to define the topic that will yield the best information before they begin any type of research, and before they look for information. Therefore, students will efficiently find the information they need.

Sample in Context: (The teacher leads the class discussion.) Knowing the "keyword topic" before beginning science research is important; however, identifying the keyword topic from a research question can be difficult. An example is given for all students to discuss and consider. The example is, "How does light effect plant growth?" Students verbally suggest the keyword topic from the research questions. Generally, students identify both *light* and *plant* as keywords. However, students need to focus on the main keyword, which in this case, is "plants." For science research, students need to identify the subject that will yield the kind of background information they will need. Next, each student looks at their individual research question written on a piece of paper and circles their keyword topic. Each student reads their research question, one at a time, out loud, and then identifies the keyword topic. This allows dialogue between the library media specialist and the student about whether or not they have selected the correct topic.

One student begins, "My research question is 'How does heat affect the bounce of a ball?' The keyword topic is ball." In defining the task, the library media specialist can illustrate that looking up the word ball in an encyclopedia does not explain how a ball bounces. However, using the keyword, "rubber" will yield the kind of background information needed. Another student might say, "My research question is 'What type of building material burns the fastest?' The keyword is fire." In this case the student is guided to several different keywords which include fire and the name of the material such as wood or plaster. The discussion continues until students have identified their keyword topic. Then they are ready for Steps 2 and 3 of the Big6, Information Seeking Strategies and Location & Access.

Title: *Learning Peers*

Author: Kathleen L. Spitzer

Related Big6 Skills: Big 6 #1—Task Definition

Purpose: Students will work together to analyze their assignment and to create a checklist of all the components.

Learning Contexts: This lesson works well when students need to organize a varietety of tasks, sub-tasks, and requirements.

Discussion: At one time or another, most students receive a complex assignment to complete; one that requires a variety of tasks. Students moan and groan as they start to read what will be required of them. They complain that it is impossible to do the assignment, and they beg us to take away some of the requirements.

Many of us have felt the same way about tasks we've had to complete. I recall getting a memo asking for an itemized list of existing furniture and a prioritized list of new furniture and equipment that would be needed for a newly renovated library media facility. In addition, it was necessary to identify how much the new items would cost. I had to prepare the list within two weeks. This seemed like an overwhelming task at first. The task was divided into several parts, and one part was assigned to each of the other two library media specialists. With the help of my co-workers a spreadsheet was completed for each area of the new facility. It was a difficult and detail-oriented task, but one that was achievable because it was divided into sub-tasks.

Students need to learn this same skill. Through the learning peers process, students work together to analyze the task and break it into manageable parts. This makes the whole task easier to face. Students can be assured that if they tackle one part at a time, the whole project will eventually be accomplished.

Item: Learning Peers (see directions and transparency masters.)

Sample in Context: Mr. Smith's social studies project was well known to most of our students and it was dreaded. The directions for the project filled four (4) pages. Students had to choose a state and:

- Create a political and topographic map
- Discuss the history of the state including when the state entered the Union
- Give the name of the current governor of the state and tell some background about him or her
- Create a poster to advertise the state
- Tell what products the state produces
- Identify any environmental problems the state may have and tell how the state is trying to handle them
- Detail the natural resources of the state
- Choose a famous person from the state and write a two-page biography of that person
- Create an advertisement for tourist attractions within the state.

The learning peers activity brought some relief to the students. After the activity, students felt more confident of their ability to tackle the project because they had a plan.

Learning Peers

Objectives: Students will work in groups of two (or more) to analyze and define a task. They will then create a checklist to evaluate their work at the completion of the task. Learning peers may help each other throughout the project as well.

Materials:
Script (see next page)
Overhead transparencies or computer-generated slides (see copy attached)

Equipment:
Computers with word processing software

Preparation:
Discuss this strategy in advance with the teacher, and ask if the teacher would consider giving the students a grade for their checklists. Enlist the teacher to play the other part in the script, and give the teacher a copy so that he or she can become familiar with it. If the teacher is reluctant, enlist a student on the day of the class.

Directions:
- Acknowledge to the class that they are facing a tough assignment with many parts.
- Note that it will be helpful to have a checklist to use for monitoring their progress.
- Tell students that they will be working with a learning peer to generate a checklist and word process it. The list will be submitted to the teacher for a grade.
- Show the rules for learning peers transparencies or slides.
- Use the script to demonstrate each aspect of a learning peer.
- Ask students to work with their learning peers to create a checklist of tasks and necessary components that will help them create an exemplary project.
- Tell students that they will use their own checklists to evaluate their projects.
- Students will then form small groups and create the word-processed checklists.

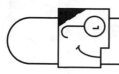

Learning Peers

A learning peer provides:

 ■ Ideas

 ■ Encouragement

A learning peer serves as a:

 ■ Timekeeper

 ■ Reminder

 ■ Editor

 ## *A learning peer does not:*
■ Do the work for you

■ React with negative criticism

■ Distract you from your work by constantly interrupting

Role Play for Learning Peers

Ideas:

Len: I can't decide on a topic for my report.

Kathy: What have you thought about doing it on?

Encouragement:

Kathy: It looks like you found a good article on El Salvador.

Timekeeper:

Len: Don't forget that tomorrow we have to move on to the next station. We should finish using this atlas today or get a pass to use the library during study hall.

Reminder:

Kathy: We're supposed to include information for a bibliography.

Editor:

Len: Would you read through the draft of my report and make suggestions?

What a learning peer does not:

Kathy: I don't feel like doing this map. How about if you make a map for me?

Len: I read through your draft last night. It really stinks.

Kathy: Did you watch *Buffy the Vampire Slayer* last night? It was great . . .

Title: *Planning Timeline*

Author: Kathleen L. Spitzer

Related Big6 Skills: Big 6 #1—Task Definition

Purpose: This exercise requires students to examine their personal calendars and to create a timeline for the completion of their project.

Learning Contexts: This lesson is appropriate for secondary or higher education students who must complete a long-term project.

Discussion: Football practice. Karate. The New Year's Semi-Formal. Part-time job. Chores. Friends. Students need to balance their lives between work and play. Some students have not learned the time management skills that allow them to schedule time to work on long-term projects. The sample schedule provides students with a plan for completing a long-term assignment and allows time for work and play.

Item: Planning Time-Line

Students should bring their personal calendars to class. The class can brainstorm any important social dates such as dances, football games, basketball games, holidays, etc. Individual class members should develop a plan for completing their project and review their plan with the teacher or library media specialist who can suggest any changes.

Sample In Context: Students in Architectural Drawing class had to:

- Create a complete floor plan for their own house
- Show an outside view of each side of their house
- Propose a renovation project for their house and provide a floor plan and outside views for that renovation

Students in the class were known to procrastinate on their assignments. They would rush into the drawing lab during their homeroom time, before school, or after school to complete a long-term assignment that should have been worked on over a period of time. For the final project of the year, the teacher decided to work with the library media specialist to design a lesson that would help students plan their time wisely. They developed the planning timeline.

Planning Timeline

Name:

Other long-range assignments due dates and time commitments:

★

Project due date:

Plan for completing this long-term project:

Note: Indicate dates by placing hash marks on the timeline.

Planning Timeline

Name:

Other long-range assignments due dates and time commitments:

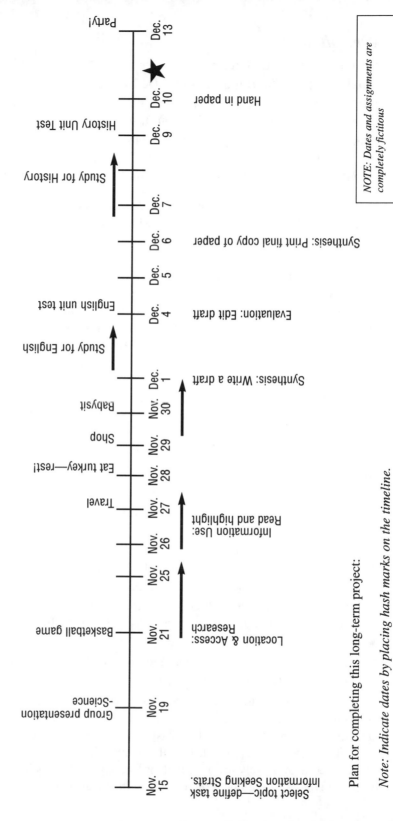

NOTE: Dates and assignments are completely fictitous

Plan for completing this long-term project:

Note: Indicate dates by placing hash marks on the timeline.

Title: *Shape It*

Author: Kathleen L. Spitzer

Related Big6 Skills: Big 6 #1—Task Definition

Purpose: This lesson provides students with a hands-on example that illustrates the importance of knowing your task.

Learning Contexts: This lesson is applicable across subject areas in secondary education settings where students have a complex assignment. This activity is especially helpful to kinesthetic learners and to reluctant learners.

Discussion: On the first day of fifth grade, our teacher gave us all tests consisting of 25 fill in the blank questions. Our class diligently filled in each blank with the information. It seemed like an easy test, and I was confident that I would do well on it. When I got to question number 25, the directions stated that I should only do question number one and then put my pencil down. Students started groaning as they got to this last question. A general hubbub arose in the room. The teacher settled us down and made the point that we should completely read through any test prior to taking it.

Similarly, students need to learn to analyze assignments and tests so they have a clear idea of what is required. The Shape It activity emphasizes the importance of knowing the requirements of an assignment. To do the activity, students work in pairs to assemble some geometric shapes (provided by the teacher) according to the directions they have received. The problem is that some of the directions are incomplete. In discussions about the activity, students conclude that knowing all of the directions is important.

Item: Shape It handout

Sample in Context: Students in a 10th grade math class were creating a report on careers that would require mathematics skills. The assignment asked the students to:

- Choose a career that they might want to pursue
- Give complete details on the job such as salary, working conditions, educational requirements, and future openings
- Find and cut out at least three (3) want ads for that job from a national newspaper or include three reprints of ads from the Internet
- Use at least three (3) sources
- Interview someone with that job and provide details about how that person uses mathematics on the job.

On the first day that students began this assignment, they came to the library to begin their research. Comments heard were: "Oh no, not another speech." "We already know how to use encyclopedias!" "Get ready to be bored...."

The library media specialist did the Shape It activity with the class and students became actively involved in their learning. They concluded that they needed to find out all of the requirements of their career project before beginning.

Shape It

Focus: *Task Definition*

The following lesson is written for a class of 32 students. Students will work in groups of two or four. It is easiest to do this lesson when students are at tables, but each pair of students can put their desks together if no tables are available. This lesson works very well for group projects.

Objective:

Students will experience working without directions.

Materials:

- Numerous geometric shapes (small, medium and large squares, rectangles, and equilateral triangles cut out of colorful poster board. (Tip: It helps if the equilateral triangles have been cut so that the sides are the same size as the sides of the squares.)
- 16 medium-size clasp envelopes
- Small strips of paper on which you have written the following sentence and two sentence fragments:

    Make an animal out of the shapes. (Make 4 copies)

    Make an (Make 4 copies)

    out of the shapes. (Make 6 copies)

Preparation:

- Divide the shapes among the 16 envelopes so that each envelope has a variety of shapes and colors
- Prepare the 16 strips of paper by following the directions above.

Directions:

- When the class is seated at tables (or you have had each pair of students put their desks together), distribute one envelope per two students. (Again, you can have four students at a table working together; however, they would have two envelopes at their table.)
- Tell the students that:
    - They will be doing an activity with the shapes that are in the envelopes
    - They will have approximately five minutes for the activity
    - The activity may prove to be frustrating, fun, or challenging depending on how they look at it
    - They may not ask any questions.
- Distribute the one slip of paper to each pair or group of students. (Try to give the real directions to students who are seated at the edges of the room so other students will not see what they are doing.)
- Tell the students to begin. (Again, if students ask any questions, explain that you cannot answer them.)
- Monitor students' reactions. Do not let students get up and wander around the room or look at what other tables have done.

- Walk around the room to observe what products the students are making.
- Stop the activity after five minutes.

At this point you have two options:

If you are short on time:

- Ask each group of students to read their directions aloud
- Look around the room and point out some examples of what each pair or group of students made. (Skip ahead to section with arrow.)

OR

If you have some time:

- Ask students to place their slips on the table below the item their group made.
- Have students walk around the room and view the creations and the directions.
➡ Ask the students who had the correct directions if they found anything frustrating about the task. They might note that they didn't have enough shapes or the right shapes to do what they wanted. If no one brings this up, you can ask if anyone had this problem.
- Ask the whole group why you had them do this activity:
    They might say:
        1. So that they could work together as a group
        2. So that they could learn what it was like to have poor directions.

If they don't bring up the point about the directions, you can say:

- Who likes to follow directions? (This works great with teens—they invariably groan!)
- Explain that you did this activity so that students would understand the importance of knowing what to do to successfully complete a task. Make the connection to the students' upcoming group projects.

Reflections

CHAPTER 7

Big6™ #2: Information Seeking Strategies

T his Chapter focuses on the second stage in the Big6 process—
Information Seeking Strategies—which has two components:

2.1 Determine all possible sources.
2.2 Select the best sources.

Once students understand their task and the information requirements of
the problem (stage #1–Task Definition), their attention should turn to the
information sources to meet the task. Teachers, students, and even teacher-
librarians sometimes talk about "seeking or finding the information needed" as
one action. However, in the Big6 approach we break this down into two
stages—first determining the most appropriate information sources for the
situation (Information Seeking Strategies) and then finding the sources and the
information in the sources (Location & Access).

Big6 TIPS: Information Seeking Strategies: Determine and Narrow

Working with students to hone their Information Seeking Strategies can be
mind-expanding and fun. We recommended a simple but powerful technique—
determine and narrow. "Determine and narrow" is used throughout the Big6

approach (for example, in Task Definition to select a topic or in Synthesis to determine an effective presentation format). "Determine and narrow" is also the essential process for Information Seeking Strategies. Here, we want students to open their minds and brainstorm all possible information sources to meet the task, and then critically determine the best sources for completing this particular task at this time.

When starting a report or paper, students typically turn to the standard sources—books, reference materials, or magazines. These may be highly appropriate, but students should also consider databases, electronic resources, community resources, experts, World Wide Web sites, businesses, various non-profit agencies, video- or audiotapes, and more. In our personal lives, we generally turn to other people for information (for example, for advice on buying a product or directions on how to get somewhere). But in school situations, we tend to look at printed or electronic sources. Our goal is to have students think broadly, to consider the full range of sources, and then select the most relevant sources for a particular task.

In developing Information Seeking Strategy skills, we first try to get students thinking as "far-out" as possible. For example, students working on assignments related to volcanoes and earthquakes might first think about encyclopedias or books on volcanoes. These are fine, but we also want them to recognize "visiting Mt. St. Helens" or "talking to a volcano expert" as possible sources. And, while in the past these might have been impractical to implement, actually locating and accessing these sources is possible today through the Internet. For example, you can visit Mt. St. Helens, The U.S. Geological Survey Website at *http://vulcan.wr.usgs.gov/Volcanoes/MSH/* or Volcano World's "Ask a Volcanologist" through *http://volcano.und.nodak.edu/vwdocs /ask_a.html.*

With more information sources available than ever before, the "narrowing" part of Information Seeking Strategies is more important than ever. Students need to learn that while there may be a number of sources to meet their needs, they must select sources carefully depending upon their situation and personal skill level. For example, a carefully written and easy-to-use encyclopedia rather than the U.S. Geological Survey Web site may better serve elementary students who know little about volcanoes. This site would be more suitable for high school seniors, while the "Volcano World" Web site is probably too general and simple for a high school senior's needs.

Rather than giving students the criteria for making selections, have them identify the criteria for determining relevant sources. You'll be pleasantly surprised when they develop a list similar to the following:

- Accuracy
- Completeness
- Reliability (is authoritative)
- Preciseness
- Validity (is on target)

- Availability
- Currency
- Ease-of-use
- Cost
- Entertainment (is fun).

Which of these criteria are most important? It all depends on the situation and the student. Is the student working on a short written assignment or a senior thesis? Is the due date next week, next month, or tomorrow? Is the student just learning to read or a highly skilled information processor?

One of the most valuable things for students to learn is that for a short homework assignment it may be fine to use readily available and easy-to-use sources such as their textbook, a slightly dated encyclopedia, or even someone's personal Web site. However, for a major report or term project they would need to use more authoritative, accurate, and complete sources such as current books, authoritative journal articles, and the Web.

Title: *Determining Criteria for Types of Resources: The Criteria Checklist*

Author: Michael B. Eisenberg

Related Big6 Skills: Big6# 2—Information Seeking Strategies

Purpose: This lesson will help students develop a clear sense of criteria for selecting sources.

Learning Contexts: Grades 7-12

Discussion: We want students to learn to make decisions about selecting sources based on criteria (e.g., accuracy, quality, authority, ease-of-use, available, current). The goal is to create a class "Criteria Checklist" that can be used throughout the school year.

Class Session 1: Creating the Criteria Checklist

- Students focus on a particular class assignment.
- The teacher makes sure the students understand the assignment and are ready to tackle Big6 #2—Information Seeking Strategies.
- Break the class into groups of 2 or 3, and give the groups five minutes to brainstorm possible types of sources [at least five] in relation to the assignment.
- The groups then select two sources that might best fulfill the assignment.
- Students write the name of each source on a card and also write "why"— why that source is the best. This is the most important part of the assignment because the "why" represents the CRITERIA for determining the most useful sources.
- Each group reports back to compile a master Criteria Checklist.
- The class should discuss and refine the list until all possible information seeking criteria are noted. The list should look something like:
  - Accurate
  - Easy-to-use
  - Complete
  - Authoritative (reliable)
  - Precise (focused)
  - On target (valid)
  - Available
  - Affordable
  - Fun.

  It's okay if the students don't get all criteria at first. Others can be added later.

- Give this list a special name, e.g., Tenth Grade Social Studies Criteria Checklist, Jackson Criteria.
- After class, write up the list in a checklist format. Consider this the "first draft."

Class session 2: Practice and Revision

- Hand out the first draft of the Criteria Checklist for review.
- Break students into groups of two to three.
- Conduct an activity where students rate various information sources in relation to assignments, based on the criteria.
- After five to ten such assignments, ask students to reconsider the criteria. Are they clear? Are any missing?

The Criteria Checklist can be continually refined so that it becomes the primary tool for the class in deciding among sources for an assignment.

Sample in Context: Mrs. Rausch, uses a range of resources—mostly electronic—to teach health. She's also "sold" on the Big6 and has integrated Big6 instruction into most of her units. For example, she uses the "Diet and Nutrition" unit to present an overview of the Big6 because it comes early in the school year and results in students creating posters that advocate good eating habits.

One of her main integrated lessons is Information Seeking Strategies—helping students recognize and select quality resources while being aware of those resources which are less useful. "Rausch's Criteria Checklist" is a mainstay of this effort. Using "finding information comparing diets" as the assignment, she works with her class to create the draft checklist. In the second session, she has students rate various electronic, print, and human sources in relation to other nutrition and health questions. The result is a refined list of criteria—Rausch's Criteria Checklist—a valuable tool to which she and the students can refer throughout the school year.

Title: *Discerning Differences*

Author: Kathleen L. Spitzer

Related Big6 Skills: Big 6 #2—Information Seeking Strategies

Purpose: In this lesson, students will identify the differences among publications. After completing this exercise, students will be able to make better decisions about which information sources to consult.

Learning Contexts: This lesson is appropriate for secondary or higher education students who conduct research.

Discussion: Different publications can approach a topic differently. For example, an article on video games published in *Time* magazine would differ from a video game article published in *GamePro*. The article in *Time* magazine might discuss the effects of video games; the article in *GamePro* might provide hints and tips to successfully play a game. Similarly, there are vast differences among Internet pages. Some are reliable and some are not. Students need to know the inherent differences among publications to become wise information users.

Item: Discerning Differences worksheet

Materials:

- A copy of a supermarket tabloid containing a splashy headline
- Discerning Differences worksheet

A great way to begin this assignment is to hold up a supermarket tabloid with a splashy (and obviously untrue) headline. You can then raise the issue of the reliability and the authority of information sources.

Here are two variations of this assignment.

Variation 1: First, the teacher or library media specialist researches one topic that will interest the class. As an option, he or she could research a topic that is related to something the class will be researching. The specialist identifies at least ten (10) sources of information on a topic from a variety of sources. Students are directed to read the article on that topic from each source and to complete the worksheet (see Discerning Differences worksheet). After the assignment is finished, the teacher and/or library media specialist can lead a discussion about the various sources and relate the discussion to Information Seeking Strategies. After this, students would begin their own research on their topic.

Variation 2: Students are given the Discerning Differences worksheet and are asked to research any topic of interest. They must find at least ten (10) different sources of information on that topic. Students should then examine these sources and note how they differ. The teacher or library media specialist can conduct a discussion about the various sources and relate this to Information Seeking Strategies. Students would continue to research the topic and finish their project.

Sample in Context: Students in English class were asked to research a current issue of their choice. The teacher noticed that some students in the past had used inappropriate resources or had used whatever resource was handy. The teacher and library media specialist decided to have the students use the Discerning Differences worksheet to encourage them to think about the sources they would choose to actually write their paper.

Name:_____ Class: _____

Discerning Differences

Title of publication:_____

Date of publication: _____

Title of story: _____

Author of story: _____

Page number(s): _____

1. Briefly summarize the information that you learned from reading this article:

2. How would you classify the type of information you read?

3. For what purposes would you use this information?

4. Examine the resource and note what other type of information in contained within it. Be specific.

Title: *Information Seeking and Brainstorming*

Author: Robert E. Berkowitz

Related Big6 Skills: Big6 #2—Information Seeking

Purpose: In this activity, students brainstorm a list of possible information sources for their research reports.

Learning Contexts: Grades 7-12

Discussion: Brainstorming is a strategy for collecting ideas by thinking freely and openly about all possibilities. Brainstorming is a cooperative group learning activity. Teaching students the rules for brainstorming will encourage them to seek both the traditional sources, as well as more creative alternative sources for their research reports.

Rules for Brainstorming:

1. Shoot for a million ideas. The goal is to collect as many ideas as possible.
2. Accept all ideas. Don't judge any ideas until you have exhausted the possibilities.
3. It's all right to be innovative. Use your imagination.
4. Expand upon ideas. Use other people's ideas as springboards for your own thinking.
5. Don't worry about spelling during the brainstorming session. Spell the best you can and keep going.
6. Don't stop... the more ideas the better... remember, shoot for a million.

Sample in Context: Mr. Lankes, a science teacher, wants his students to learn how to develop a list of specific terms they can use when searching the Web for information on classification systems.

He gives his students a "pre-thinking" homework assignment to list 10 vocabulary words that relate to the term classification. Knowing that there are a lot of terms, he begins class the next day by having students share their lists. He decides to allow students to use the brainstorming technique to generate more ideas. Using the brainstorming strategy, he asks students to list as many new words as possible.

Students are excited about contributing to the discussion. They create a long list of possibilities. Some of their ideas and terms are traditional, some are fanciful, but all are ways to describe classification.

Mr. Lankes divides his class into small groups. Each group gets a list of terms to use to search the Web. The goal is to determine if the terms will result in hits that relate to science classification schemes. Students keep a search log of their strategy and outcome to share with the rest of the class.

As a closure activity for this lesson, Mr. Lankes uses the brainstormed list to highlight those organization or classification terms that are most often used in science and how they are used.

Title: *Information Seeking Strategies on the Web*

Author: Robert Darrow

Related Big6 Skills: Big6 #2—Information Seeking Strategies

Purpose: This lesson helps students learn which World Wide Web search mechanisms will yield the best information.

Learning Contexts: Grades 5–12

Discussion: After students learn how hyperlinks work, students need to learn how to find information on the Web. It is important to put this in the context of the Big6 because then students realize that finding and using information on the Web is no different than finding and using information from a book. To use information effectively, students need to know the difference between a variety of search mechanisms available on the World Wide Web. There is not one search mechanism that will find all of the best information on any one topic on the World Wide Web. Students need to learn how to judiciously choose search mechanisms that will yield the kind of information needed for any particular topic. Learning how to find information on the Web is an essential skill for all students. Learning how different search mechanisms operate will help students find pertinent information.

Item: Web Search Mechanisms worksheet; Web Search Guide (URL: *http://www.itrc.ucf.edu*); B6 Web Chart.

Note: Have at least one computer connected to the Internet for every two students for this lesson. This lesson is workable in small groups as well.

Begin by giving students the "Web Search Mechanisms Worksheet." Explain to students that some of the major search mechanisms on the World Wide Web are: Hot Bot (*http://www.hotbot.com*), Alta Vista (*http://www.altavista.com*), and Yahoo (*http://www.yahoo.com*). Metasearch engines include: Mamma (*http://www.mamma.com*), Dogpile (*http://www.dogpile.com*) and Metacrawler (*http://www.metacrawler.com*). One other search that operates a bit differently than others is NorthernLight (*http://www.northernlight.com*). These search mechanisms will continue to be refined and improved, and other new search mechanisms will be even more effective at finding information on the Web. These are the major search mechanisms at the time of this publication.

Knowing which search engine to use in a given situation means applying Big6 Skill #2, Information Seeking Strategies, to the World Wide Web. Students need to identify a topic before beginning this search process. For example, students might want to find information about an African American scientist or a certain event in history. To learn how different search mechanisms work, students need to use at least four different search mechanisms. Students also need to be able to explain how each search mechanism displays the information. Students will explore the different search mechanisms by going to that site, typing in a keyword and then viewing the results. (Remind students that during Information Seeking Strategies, they are learning about the search mechanisms, not actually going to a certain Web site).

Students need to answer the questions, "How is the information displayed?" In other words, "does the search mechanism list words, or brief descriptions of Web sites?" "Is there something that tells users if the information on a certain Web site is reliable?"

Students may begin with any search mechanism on the worksheet as long as they view all of them. Younger students might use only Yahoo, Alta Vista, Dogpile and NorthernLight. Write the Web addresses on the board for students or create a Web page with the hyperlinked search mechanisms. The teacher needs to demonstrate the type of information students should complete. For example, if the student uses Yahoo, one might write in the Web address column: "http://www.yahoo.com." In the "description" column, the student might write: "list of words or brief description of Web site. No hits listed. No author listed." Students learn that Yahoo is actually a directory of Web sites organized by subject words. In Alta Vista, students learn that Web sites are listed by the name of the Web site with a brief description. In Dogpile, information is displayed by different search mechanisms. Other differences between search mechanisms include how the number of hits are displayed, how the Web sites are ordered, and how much information is summarized. Finally, students learn that for an exhaustive search on a topic, using a metasearch engine would yield the best results.

Sample in Context: Students who are learning to use the World Wide Web may apply this process in any subject area and in any learning context.

This method allows students to find information they need in a more efficient and successful way.

Student success in this process is measured by how well each student can verbalize how each search mechanism displays information. Students can either verbally share this information with one another, write notes about each Web site, or share the information with the entire class. Once students learn about various search mechanisms, they are able to move on to the next step of the Big6, Location & Access.

Web Search Mechanisms Worksheet
Big6™ - Information Seeking Strategies on the Web

Search Mechanism	Web Address	How is information displayed? (short descriptions? How many hits? Author listed?)
Yahoo		
AltaVista		
NorthernLight		
HotBot		
Dogpile		
Mamma		
Metacrawler		

Created by Rob Darrow, February, 1998

Web Search Guide — Which Search Mechanisms Do What....

Created by Donna Baumbach and Mary Bird
University of Central Florida
Instructional Technology Resource Center
On the Web at: http://www.itrc.ucf.edu
Updated and enhanced by Robert Darrow, July, 1998

Do you want to...	...Then try these tools!			
Browse a broad topic	Yahoo **www.yahoo.com/**	Magellan **http://magellan.excite.com**	Starting Point **www.stpt.com/**	
Browse educational topics and resources	Schrockguide **http://school.discovery.com/ schrockguide**	Connections + (MCREL) **http://www.mcrel.org/ standards-benchmarks/**	Study Web **http://www.studyweb.com**	
Search largest amount of Internet *(meta-search engines)*	Metacrawler **www.metacrawler.com/**	SavvySearch **http://www.search.com**	Dogpile **www.dogpile.com/**	Mamma **www.mamma.com**
Search for a narrow topic	AltaVista **www.altavista.com/**	HotBot **http://hotbot.lycos.com/**	Excite **www.excite.com/**	go.com **http://go.com**
Search using natural language	Electric Monk **www.electricmonk.com**	Ask Jeeves **www.askjeeves.com**	Research Paper.Com **www.researchpaper.com**	
Do a unique search	NorthernLight (Searches grouped words) **http://www.northernlight.com/**	Semio Search (concept mapping) **http://www.semio.com**	Open Text Index (Word based search) **http://www.opentext.com**	
Search only reviewed sites	Magellan **http://magellan.excite.com**	Argus Clearinghouse **www.clearinghouse.net/**		
Search specific types of databases	Four11 **www.four11.com/**	MapQuest **www.mapquest.com/**	Research-It! **www.itools.com/research-it/**	

Internet Search Tools Quick Reference Guide

	AltaVista (Simple Search) www.altavista.com	AltaVista (Advanced Search) www.altavista.com	HotBot www.hotbot.com	Excite www.excite.com	go.com http://go.com	Magellan www.mckinley.com	Yahoo www.yahoo.com
And	+cats +pets	cats AND pets	cats AND pets	cats AND pets +cats +pets	+cats +pets	cats AND pets	+cats + pets
Or	cats kittens	cats OR kittens	cats OR kittens	cats OR kittens	cats, kittens	cats OR kittens	Use Options
Not	+cats -wild	cats AND NOT wild wild	cats AND NOT wild wild	cats AND NOT wild +cat -wild	+cats -wild	cats AND NOT wild +cats -wild	+cats -wild
Exact phrase	"pet care"	"pet care"	"pet care"	"pet care"	"pet care"	"pet care"	"pet care"
Complex Searching	Use advanced search —>	(cats or kittens) AND NOT wild	N/A	(cats or kittens) AND NOT wild	N/A	(cats or kittens) AND NOT wild	N/A
Truncation/ Wild Card	Use advanced search —>	cat*	cat*	Automatic suffixes	N/A	N/A	cat*

Title: *Information Seeking Strategy: Higher-Order Thinking Skills*

Author: Robert E. Berkowitz

Related Big6 Skills: Big6 #2—Information Seeking Strategies

Purpose: This worksheet incorporates higher order thinking skills into Information Seeking Strategies. Students can prioritize sources by applying specific criteria such as timelines, authority, readability, and so forth.

Learning Contexts: Grades 7-12

Discussion: This generic worksheet may be used in a variety of instructional units where the school library media specialist and/or classroom teacher want to focus students' attention on Information Seeking Strategies. Simple to use, the worksheet asks for a "YES" or "NO" response and their reason why a source might be useful to their assignment. Obviously, the focus of this worksheet is on Information Seeking Strategies, Big6 # 2.2—select the best sources.

Item: Higher-Order Thinking Skills worksheet

Sample in Context: Mrs. Wenzel has created an assignment for students to learn about the impact an artist's life on their creative work. After assigning the task, students become engaged in Information Seeking Strategies, looking for resources that will potentially help them complete their report. To assist her students, Mrs. Wenzel hands out an Information Seeking Strategy worksheet. The worksheet helps students focus attention on the potential sources and which ones are best for the assignment. Additionally, the worksheet allows students to keep a work strategy log while they prepare their working bibliography.

As students complete the worksheet, they consider and apply specific criteria for each source they think will be helpful in their research effort. Such criteria may include: readability, relevance, and the authority of the author.

Before moving on to the note-taking stage (Information Use), Mrs. Wenzel checks each students' work. She also takes time to review with students the reasons why some information sources are better than others.

Information Seeking Strategies
Higher-Order Thinking Skills Worksheet

Student: _____

Class: _____

Topic: _____

1. Write the bibliographic citation of all the sources you think might be useful for your report or project.

2. Put a check in the "YES" box if the source has information on your topic that will be helpful in writing your report.

3. Put a check in the "NO" box if the source has no information about your topic.

4. List your reason for including or excluding the sources for use on your paper or project.

Yes	No	Citation	Reason

Reflections

CHAPTER 8

Big6™ #3: Location & Access

Stage three of the Big6 process, **Location & Access**, has two components:

    3.1 Locate sources.
    3.2 Find information within sources.

Location & Access, the focus of most traditional "library skills" curricula, are clearly important skills. However, with the Big6 and other process-oriented approaches, we now recognize that Location & Access skills are part of a broader process. Once students understand their task and brainstorm and select the most appropriate source to use for the situation, it's now time to actually get the source and the relevant information from within the source.

Big6 TIPS: Location & Access–
Think Index, Keywords, and Boolean

In the Big6 approach, we like to think about Location & Access from a top-down perspective. That is, rather than jump into the details, we prefer to focus on the big concepts and skills. With Location & Access, for example, there's a tendency to get caught up with teaching the mechanics of search commands, the use of guidewords or other aids, or the features of an online catalog or database system. Certainly these aspects are important, but students first need to understand and appreciate the big picture.

    For Location & Access, that means the concept of **Index**. Say the word out loud— **Index**. Comforting, isn't it? Librarians love indexes—and with good reason. Indexes are the key to effective and efficient information searching. Indexes make it possible to find useful information in books, databases, and even in that most massive of information stores—the World Wide Web. So, before we work with students on skills related to the specific use of indexes, we first want them to appreciate and seek out indexes. Here's a sample exercise for teaching this—to have students recognize and value indexes:

Explain the concept of "index" to the class. Explain about sequential access to information—looking through a book page by page or browsing through a database record by record. Then explain the point of an index—an "inverted file" that organizes the content alphabetically for easy searching and location.

Show the class some common indexes—the index in the back of their science book, the library catalog, or the index to the encyclopedia. Make sure they understand the concept.

Now challenge them to identify indexes in everyday life. You give them the type of information, and they have to note the index. For example:

Telephone – the phone book

Stores in a shopping mall – the directory

Television shows – the TV guide in the newspaper

Candy in a supermarket – the videotext system.

There are plenty of these. Challenge them to stump you as well.

The point is to help students realize that if they really want to save time and effort in locating and accessing information—find the index. Another way to teach the idea of **Index** is to use the World Wide Web and search engines. Divide the class, but only let one group use a search engine, the other must browse; then switch. They will quickly see why Yahoo and the other search engines are so popular. You can expand on this by testing the different search engines. Have the class attempt to search for the same topic, but with different groups using different search engines. Let students set the criteria (number of hits, speed, ease-of-use, information displayed, etc.), run the tests, and make the comparisons. I've done this with students as young as fourth grade, and I was amazed at their insights.

A discussion of search engines often leads to considering search strategies and keywords. Using Indexes and keyword search strategies are both essential skills for Location & Access. However, research shows that students rarely consider alternative terms when searching for information. They are more likely to change their topic than try synonyms! So, discuss what a synonym is (you'll be amazed at what you hear), and try to get them to expand their thinking and brainstorm various alternatives to represent the topic they are seeking. Use graphic organizers (charts and mind maps) to facilitate brainstorming keywords.

Finally, there's the matter of Boolean searching. In electronic indexes, search results can be expanded by linking terms with a Boolean term, "or." Conversely, results can be narrowed with a Boolean term, "and." Students readily grasp these concepts when they are searching a magazine index or the Web. But remember the top-down approach: students are ready for learning about Boolean operators only after they fully grasp the concept of index and the value of keywords.

Title: *Big6™ Location Log*

Author: Robert E. Berkowitz
Related Big6 Skill: Big6 #3—Location & Access

Discussion: This location log is a follow-up to the Information Seeking Strategies Worksheet on page 102. Specifically designed for use with the Web, students may use this log to record sites that best meet their information needs.

Big6™ Location Log

Assignment:

Date	Source	URL/Call Number/Brief Citation	Keyword(s)	Usefulness

Title: *Internet Search Tips: Keys to Effective Internet Searching*

Author: Robert E. Berkowitz
Related Big6 Skills: Big6 #1—Task Definition, Big6 #2—Information Seeking Strategies, Big6 #3—Location & Access, Big6 #4—Information Use

Purpose: This *PowerPoint* presentation prepares students to search the Internet using truncation, distinctive words, or Boolean operators.

Learning Contexts: Grades 7-12

Discussion: It helps to know a few tricks and tips for efficient Internet searching. This *PowerPoint* presentation teaches students how to maximize their time and effort by using specific searching techniques.

Item: Internet Search Tips: Keys to Effective Internet Searching (*PowerPoint* handout).

Internet Search Tips:
Task Definition

+ Clearly define your information need.
+ What do you need/want to know?
+ How much information do you need/want?
+ Hint: Use general library resources, such as encyclopedias, other reference and non-fiction books before you begin using the Internet.

Internet Search Tips:
Information Seeking Strategies

+ Does your topic. . . Have distinctive words or phrases?
+ If your topic does have distinctive words or phrases, then enclose the word(s) or phrase(s) in "quotes".
+ Example: "coronary heart disease"

Internet Search Tips: Location & Access

✦ Carefully select your search terms.

✦ Use synonyms, alternates, broader and/or narrower search terms to expand or narrow your search if necessary.

Internet Search Tips: Location & Access

✦ If your topic has no distinctive words or phrases then your search requires more than one term with AND or +.

✦ Example: health and wellness

Internet Search Tips: Location & Access

✦ Use advanced search techniques such as truncation & Boolean logic.

✦ Truncation is used to expand results.

✦ A common truncation symbol is * (asterisk).

Internet Search Tips: Location & Access

✦ Use the truncation search technique. Truncation: * (asterisk)

✦ For example, a search on the word child* would also search for: childish, children, children's

Internet Search Tips: Location & Access

✦ Use the Boolean logic search technique. Boolean logic enables a searcher to define sets and search on sets using Boolean operators.

✦ The principal Boolean operators are: AND (intersection), OR (union), NOT (difference).

Internet Search Tips: Location & Access

✦ Use the Boolean logic search technique.

Pizza or Pepperoni

Pizza

Pizza and Mushrooms not Pepperoni

Pizza and Pepperoni and Mushrooms

Pepperoni

Mushrooms

Internet Search Tips:
Location & Access
Information Use

+ When searching the Internet you may need to vary your approach.
+ Carefully and accurately record your findings.
+ Carefully organize your bookmarks within meaningful headings.

Internet Search Tips:
Information Seeking Strategy

+ Don't bog down in any search strategy that doesn't work.

+ Get help whenever you need it.

Title: *Keyword Generator: A Tool to Boost Use of Keywords*

Author: Robert E. Berkowitz and Michael B. Eisenberg

Related Big6 Skills: Big6 # 3—Location & Access

Purpose: Students will learn to brainstorm and organize keywords.

Learning Contexts: This lesson is appropriate for middle, secondary, or college-age students who need to further develop their search skills.

Discussion: The Keyword Generator is a tool for Location & Access—to use when teaching students how to conduct better searchers. Often, students have trouble generating vocabulary terms for searching. And even when they do come up with some key terms, they may not consider how various terms relate to each other. The Keyword Organizer provides a framework for helping students to think through their topics, relevant keywords, and connections among the words. Optimizing vocabulary is especially important when using the Web, because many search engines do not have a controlled vocabulary for more precise searching.

Teaching keyword searching (or any other Big6 Skill) should only take place in the context of an assignment. Here's a tool to use when working with a group about to look for information in electronic and print resources.

Potential situations might be:

- 8th graders searching the Web for information to write biographies of current newsmakers

- 11th graders working on a unit about "war"—using a variety of print, electronic, and online resources to study the causes, nature, and effects of particular wars

- High school economics students looking for strategic intelligence on various corporations

- A community college course social issues class studying "intellectual property in the information age" and looking for copyright regulations across types of media.

Sample in Context: One major unit in Mr. Robinson's economics class focuses on the stock market and making good investment decisions. The unit spans the entire year and focuses on competitive intelligence and the use of quality information.

In the beginning of the school year, Mr. Robinson helps the students to determine the major aspects for investigation related to various companies and industries, e.g., products, finances, markets, competitors, etc.

The students enter these aspects as "subtopics" in the Keyword Generator and brainstorm synonyms that also describe each subtopic. For example, for the keyword subtopic "finances," they generate:

- Budget
- Income and expenses
- Balance sheet
- Assets
- Sales
- Funds.

   After trying some of these terms in searching the Web and the full-text magazine and newspaper databases, the students reflect on which terms were most useful. If they need to continue their searching, they can revise their Keyword Generator or add subtopics that further focus their searching.

Access: Keyword Searching

The key to access within a resource is the <u>vocabulary.</u> The following exercise will help to develop a rich vocabulary for searching on a particular topic.

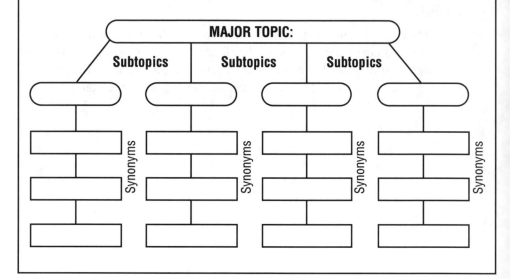

Title: *Locating Information on the Web*

Author: Robert Darrow

Related Big6 Skills: #3—Location & Access

Purpose: This lesson will help students learn how to find and save Web sites for a research topic.

Learning Contexts: Grades 5–12

Discussion: First, students need to learn how to use a Web search mechanism. Next, they need to learn how to locate reliable Web sites and make sure that the Web site contains the needed information. It is critical for students to learn various steps for finding needed information on the Web, even if they do have concentrated time to search the Web. For shorter amounts of time, these steps may be introduced one at a time so students can learn this process during several sessions. Students who simply go to a certain Web site will not gain the valuable skills they will need when they begin searching the Internet on their own.

This process is successful with students any time they are using the World Wide Web to find sources of information. This lesson works best if there is at least one computer for every two students, and if each computer is connected to the Internet.

First decide which Web search mechanism to use in Big6 Step #2, Information Seeking Strategies. The next step is Big6 Step #3, Locating & Accessing the information needed. This step is critical in helping students to focus. Remind students that in Location & Access, they are simply finding from three to five Web sites that might have information they need. (This is much like looking in the index of a book). Students will view a pre-determined number of Web sites depending upon the age of students, the amount of time, and the subject of the project.

The process of finding Web pages begins by choosing a search mechanism, typing in a keyword, and then looking at the "search results" page. The specific Location & Access steps are as follows:

1. View the "front page" of several Web sites. When looking at the Web site, students need to ask two questions:
   - Will this Web site show me information I need for my topic?
   - Is this information from a reliable source?
2. If the answer is NO, then click on the "Back" button, go to the search page and look at the next Web site.
3. If the answer is YES, Bookmark the site or mark the site as a Favorite, then go "Back" to the search page.
4. Repeat this process until an adequate number of Web sites are found.

This searching process can be accomplished in a relatively short amount of time. Next, students can proceed to Big6 Step 4, Use of Information, or they can save Bookmarks or Favorites to a disk for later use.

Item: B6 Web Chart handout

Sample in Context: This process of finding and looking at Web sites can be applied in any subject area when students need to find information on the World Wide Web. Students learn a process for finding and saving World Wide Web sites that can be applied in any learning context.

Student success is measured by the list of Bookmarks or Favorites they create. The teacher or library media teacher looks at each student's list of Bookmarks. Teachers show students how to save these Bookmarks and Favorites to a disk for later use.

For larger research projects, students need to learn how to organize Bookmarks or Favorites within dividers and folders.

Surf the Web With the Big6™

Information Problem-Solving Process	Searching the World Wide Web	Examples
Task Definition	■ What are my best search terms? ■ Use the most common term(s) first. ■ Should I use "quotes" to find exact phrases? ■ Should I use an asterisk to broaden my search process? ■ Use of Boolean terms.	▶ Greece, Ancient Greece Narrow Search: "Greek History" Expand Search: Greec* Boolean terms: and, or, not
Information Seeking Strategies	■ Which search engine will find the information I need? ■ For suggestions, the University of Central Florida has provided a guide: http://www.itrc.ucf.edu/conferences/pres/bookmark.html	▶ AltaVista (http://*altavista.com*) ▶ NorthernLight (http://*www.northernlight.com*) ▶ Yahoo (http://*www.yahoo.com/*) ▶ Dogpile (http://*www.dogpile.com/*) ▶ AskJeeves (http://*www.askjeeves.com*)
Location & Access	■ Do a search. Look at search results. ■ Click to see Web sites. ■ Skim Web sites. ■ Bookmark/Mark Favorites as important ones. ■ Save to disk.	Saving bookmarks in Netscape: ▶ Go to Windows menu, save. Saving favorites in Microsoft Explorer: ▶ Go to Favorites menu, save.
Use of Information	■ Open bookmarked Web sites. ■ Read each Web site to find information. ■ Save important text to word processing program. ■ Include title of Web site and Web address for bibliography. ■ Save text document and/or pictures.	**Save Text:** Highlight text, copy text, open word processing program, paste text and save to disk. **Pictures:** Right click (Win) or click and hold (Mac) Highlight "save image as." Save to hard drive or disk.
Synthesis	■ Word processing document with Web pages documented. ■ Important text and pictures saved for later use.	Can be printed or stored on disk for later use.
Evaluation	■ Which search engine worked best for me? Why? ■ Did this process work for me? Why or why not? ■ Did I get the information I wanted?	

Big6™ Web Guide created by Robert Darrow (Robdarrow@aol.com), Library Media Teacher, Alta Sierra Intermediate School Clovis, CA11/97, Updated 2/98.

*Based on the Big6™ created by Mike Eisenberg and Bob Berkowitz.

Title: *Using a Search Engine to Find Information: Which One is Best?*

Author: Robert E. Berkowitz

Related Big6 Skills: Big6 #3—Location & Access

Purpose: This activity will help students discover the strengths and weaknesses of different search engines.

Learning Contexts: Grades 7-12

Discussion: It's important to be able to locate and access information efficiently and effectively. This is especially true when searching for information on the Web. Each search engine is different and one may locate more appropriate resources than another search engine. Comparing different search engines allows students to learn their differences, strengths, and weaknesses.

Item: Search Engine worksheet

Sample in Context: Mrs. Drake's health class has a project to do. As part of their assignment on heart disease, they're interested in learning about Web search engines as a way to locate and access information. Using the Search Engine worksheet and their textbook, each student begins to work on their topic by determining related search terms. Searching the Web with at least three search engines for each term, students compare results. The criteria they use include usefulness and currency. They also compare the search engines based upon the number of sites found and the site summary.

Back in class, students discuss their search results and come to consensus on the best search engine for this assignment.

Search Engine Worksheet

Topic: _____

Search Terms:

Place an "X" in the chart below for each statement that applies.

My search results were:	AltaVista	Yahooligans	Excite	KidsClick!	Other:
relevant					
useful					
categorized					
ranked					
current					

It was easy to find:					
The number of sites found					
A site summary					
The URL–address					

Reflections

CHAPTER 9

Big6™ #4: Use of Information

S tage four of the Big6 process is Use of Information. **Use of Information** has two components:

4.1 Engage (read, hear, view) the information in a source.
4.2 Extract relevant information.

Big6 TIPS: Use of Information–
Where the Rubber Meets the Road

Use of Information marks a major shift in focus in the information problem-solving process. Previously, most of the Big6 action revolved around finding information sources to match information needs. But now, things change—from selecting and accessing sources to using information itself. This is "wherethe rubber meets the road" because it requires heavy-duty "critical thinking" as students engage the information in a source (Ann Irving from England calls this "interrogating an information source") in order to recognize relevant information (Big6 #4.1). The challenge is to extract the relevant information through some form of note-taking.

Engaging information involves reading and media comprehension and is the heart of what we mean by literacy. This is a major concern of classroom teachers, particularly language arts and reading teachers. However, teacher-librarians can also help students learn effective Use of Information skills by working with students on:

- Recognizing where comprehension fits in the overall information problem-solving process
- Skimming and scanning techniques, and
- Identifying relevant information.

For example, relevance is more than simply "being on a topic." There are degrees of relevance based on the original charge (Task Definition) and how the student will present the result (Synthesis). In her dissertation on user criteria of relevance, Carol Barry (1994) found that people base relevance decisions on: recency, depth/scope, accuracy, clarity, and novelty. Here's a technique for teaching students to recognize and apply relevance criteria:

Before students are about to use information resources related to their own tasks, give students an information problem and a one-page reading that addresses that problem. Ask them to highlight the passages that they think are relevant to the problem. Then ask them to go back and explain why they selected the passages. Compare their reasons to Barry's criteria. Finally, using a different colored highlighter, have them go over the reading again. You may want to do this more than once before having the students begin working on their own tasks.

It is also important to assess whether students are able to engage and identify relevant information before we ask them to extract, combine, and present information. This isn't always clear in schools. For example, when completing a typical homework assignment—answering questions at the end of a chapter—we ask students to answer the question in their own words. That's fine, but what we are really doing is asking them to locate, access, engage, extract, organize, and present—that's Big6 numbers 3 through 5 all at once! If they get the wrong answer, how do you know if the problem was in getting to the right place in the textbook (Big6 #3) or understanding the content (Big6 #4) or writing the answer in their own words (Big6 #5). I believe you've got to "walk before you can run." So, try this:

Early in the school year, just focus on engage (Big6 #4.1) and extract (Big6# 4.2). When the students are doing that typical homework assignment, forget about putting the answer in their own words. Put the answer in direct quotes and cite the page(s) where the quote appears. That will help classroom teachers and teacher-librarians assess whether students are able to comprehend the information (engage) and identify the relevant sections (extract). Later, the students can work on using their own words, the Synthesis part.

The point is to go beyond simply expecting students to be able to comprehend and use information. Classroom teachers, librarians, and reading specialists need to work together to help students improve their ability to sift through lots of information and recognize what's relevant to their specific task, problem, or need.

After developing Big6 #4.1–Engage (read, hear, view) the information in a source, we need to pay specific attention to Big6 #4.2–Extract relevant information.

Librarians and classroom teachers have taught classic note-taking skills for many years. This usually involves some form of the "note-card" method—writing single ideas from a source on a 3x5 card along with a notation that links the card to the full citation for the source. Information about the sources is usually stored on cards as well—the bibliography cards.

Why teach the note-card method? Is it an efficient way to take notes from a source? If teacher-librarians were asked to write a scholarly paper on some topic, would they use the note-card method themselves? Probably not. That's because the note-card method is actually not designed for efficient note-taking—it's designed for efficient organization of information *after* all the notes are available. Therefore, note-cards help with Big6 Skill #5.1–organization of information, not #4.2–extraction.

That's not to say we should abandon the note-card method. It just means that we should be clear about our reasons for using the method. The key to the note-card method is this business of using only one card per main idea, point, or concept. If students write more than one idea on a card, they've defeated the whole purpose for using the method. But, students often do write more than one idea on a card because they don't want to "waste" space on cards! So, it's critical to make sure students understand the purpose of the note-cards if they are going to use this method.

But, let's consider alternatives to the note-card method. Again, what would you do if you were given the task of extracting information for a scholarly paper? Well, in college, most of us probably used some form of the "photocopy-highlight" method of extraction of information. We went to the library and used the catalog or periodical indexes to identify relevant books and journal articles (Big6 #3.1), located the important sections in the books and articles (Big6 #3.2), and took a quick look to make sure that the sections contained what we wanted (Big6 #4.1). Then we made photocopies of all the pages we wanted to use. That's extraction of information—Big6 #4.2. We would also make sure that we noted the full citation of the source on the front page of the photocopied page. Later, we would go back and read the copies in detail (Big6 #4.1), highlighting specific sections that we wanted to use (Big6 #4.2). And finally, we would use some method for taking that information and organizing it for our paper (Big6 #5.1). This might involve marking up the highlighted sections using some form of coding scheme related to the outline of our paper or rewriting the notes according to a draft outline of the paper (Big6 #5.2). Today, most of us would use word processing software to assist with this endeavor.

Computer-based information resources and processing capabilities offer new opportunities and challenges for Use of Information and Synthesis. For example, many teachers and teacher-librarians complain that all the students do is print out everything—without even thinking about whether they are going to use the information. Let's look at this more carefully. First, there may be good reasons for printing out everything; perhaps there are only a few limited computer stations and other students want to use them. Second, reading text on a screen can become tedious. You try it—would you rather read page after page on the screen or print it out and read it later? Lastly, printing out is not all that different from photocopying—except we were paying by the page so we took some time to make sure that the sections we copied were ones we wanted to use. So, let's do the same with students—have them quickly skim the screen to make sure the sections they are printing are relevant to their needs.

We also need to follow-up on techniques for highlighting and organizing the information once it is printed out. How about offering instruction on identifying relevant information within text. Give all students the same article, highlighters, and a topic to study. See what they highlight and if they agree. Chances are they will highlight too much. So work on this with more examples and different colored highlighters. Also help students learn how to work totally on the computer—going from an online source, to highlight and copy on screen, to paste into a word processing program. Having a rough outline of the paper in advance can greatly enhance this process, and don't forget to work with them on time-saving techniques of keeping track of citations for the sections they copied and pasted.

Students also need to learn how to extract relevant information from other forms of information besides print and electronic. Consider offering lessons (always in the context of real assignments and curriculum) in relation to human sources (interview note-taking, audio recording), television (video recording), observation (photography, video recording, field notes), and other forms of multimedia. We talk about the changing information landscape so let's make sure our students are prepared for it.

Title: *Bits and Pieces*

Author: Sandra Baker and Kathleen L. Spitzer

Related Big6 Skills: Big6 #4—Information Use

Purpose: In this exercise, students will extract "bits and pieces" of information through guided note-taking.

Learning Contexts: This lesson is appropriate for middle school students or for high school students who have difficulty extracting information.

Discussion: We've all heard it—teachers lamenting that they received yet another research paper or project that seems to contain sections that have been copied wholesale from the source—and without proper credit. Some students have not learned techniques to identify and extract the pertinent parts of articles, books, and videos. Guided note-taking can help students do just that: identify and extract pertinent information and give proper credit to the source if a direct quote is used.

For guided note-taking, the teacher identifies the type of information that the student will seek and provides a note-taking template for the student to use. There are several ways to create a template. The teacher can develop an outline, a chart, or a mind map. Figures 1, 2, and 3 provide samples of three types of note-taking templates about U.S. immigration.

An optional way to develop note-taking templates is to have the students brainstorm the major headings as a group and then allow them to choose the style of template that they would like to create for their own use.

Sample in Context: It was time for Mr. Sobo's 11th grade students to prepare a report on the life of a poet, include and analyze examples of their major works, and identify the poet's major contributions to literature. Since students had already completed other research projects prior to this one, Mr. Sobo knew that some students would be able to identify the information that they would need for the report, while others would need some extra coaching.

This year, Mr. Sobo decided to try something different. He paired up the students so that each pair had a student with strong note-taking skills and a student who had note-taking skills that needed improvement. He explained to the students that their first task for the project was to read the directions for the assignment and design a customized note-taking template. The students were shown a variety of note-taking templates and were asked to work with their partners to decide the sub-headings under which they would record their notes. He told the students that they would test their templates on a generic example to see if their design and sub-headings were working well.

As students worked together in pairs to identify sub-headings, Mr. Sobo walked around the room to monitor their progress and to make suggestions. He then distributed a short article about Robert Frost and instructed the pairs of students to take notes on the article using their templates. He reminded students that they were to record "bits and pieces" of information and not whole sentences unless they were particularly meaningful and were to be used as direct quotes. He told the students to record the appropriate bibliographic information for the source. He demonstrated how he would take notes for the first paragraph using a template that he had constructed. Then he asked the class to take notes on the second and third paragraphs. Again, he moved about the classroom monitoring the progress of the students.

Mr. Sobo was pleased with the result of the lesson. The students seemed to be much better prepared to take meaningful notes rather than copy whole sections.

Bits and Pieces –Example Worksheets

Figure 1. Immigrant Group

   I. Time Period
  II. Region
 III. Reasons for Immigration
     A.
     B.
     C.
 IV. Areas of Settlement
     A.
     B.
     C.
  V. Laws and Restrictions
     A.
     B.
     C.
 VI. Problems Encountered
     A.
     B.
     C.
VII. Contributions
     A.
     B.
     C.

Figure 2. U .S. History

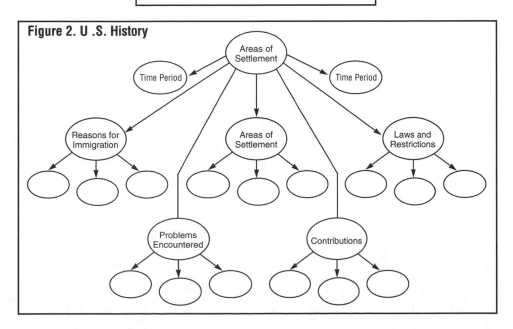

Figure 3. U.S. History
Immigrant Group Name:
Region:

Time Period/Dates	Reasons for Immigration	Areas of Settlement
Laws and Restrictions	**Problems Encountered**	**Contributions**

Title: *Connecting with People: Interview for Information*

Author: Robert E. Berkowitz

Related Big6 Skill: Big6# 4—Information Use

Learning Contexts: Grades 7-12. An interview is an important information gathering technique. Here are some Big6 guidelines that your students can use to conduct a successful interview.

Discussion: We often forget that people are a good source of information. The key is to teach students to be prepared. Preparation for an interview involves more than simply locating a person and asking them random questions to which the answers are simply "yes" or "no." To be successful interviewers, students need a strategy.

Before:

- Locate a person who is a subject matter expert in your topic.
- Arrange for an appointment. Tell your "expert" why you want to interview him or her, and explain the topics you want to discuss.
- Let your expert know if they need to prepare for the interview and, if so, what to prepare.
- Get permission to video- or audio-tape the interview.
- Thank your expert in advance for agreeing to be interviewed.
- Prepare your questions ahead of time Make a complete set of questions. Your questions should include general questions to relax your "expert" as well as specific questions about your topic. Remember to avoid asking questions that can be answered with "yes" or "no."

During:

- Arrive on time.
- Begin by thanking your expert for agreeing to participate in the interview.
- Be an active listener. Be attentive and interested in the responses.
- Start your interview with your prepared questions. Follow your general questions with more detailed questions, but don't debate with your expert.
- Take good notes even if you are recording the interview session.
- Stay within the time schedule you agreed to when you made your appointment.
- Thank your expert at the end of the interview.

After:

- Write up your notes as soon after the interview as possible.
- When you are done, check back with the expert about any additional facts you may need or questions you may have.
- Write a personal thank-you note to your expert.

Title: *Diamond Thinking*

Author: Robert E. Berkowitz

Related Big6 Skills: Big6 #4—Use of Information

Purpose: In this activity, students associate their ideas with the information they find.

Learning Contexts: Grades 6–12. Diamond Thinking is an Information Use strategy that helps students become divergent thinkers. This activity encourages students to expand their ideas as they engage and extract information from material they read, hear, or view.

Discussion: Ask students to list information from their research in the "Information" diamond (left diamond). Students then respond to that information by writing their thoughts in the "My Thoughts" diamond (right diamond). Information in the "My Thoughts" diamond may be based upon personal opinion or experience. In addition, students may fill in the "My Thoughts" with questions that were not answered by information they read, heard, or viewed.

Variation: One variation is to switch the headings and make "My Thoughts" in the left diamond, and Information in the right column. Using this variation, students begin by listing their ideas and opinions, and through research, complete the right diamond with information that validates or disputes their opinion.

Item: Diamond Thinking handout

Sample in Context: Students in Mr. Lake's 12th grade health class are working on a communicable diseases unit. Mr. Lake's assignment includes accessing and locating information on the Web about communicable diseases. To help students personalize the experience, he uses the "Diamond Thinking" strategy.

As students locate and read web-based information on their topics from the pre-selected sites, they complete the left diamond with four facts that relate to how the disease is transmitted. These facts are placed in the "Information" diamonds.

Students respond with their opinion or personal experience in the corresponding right "My Thoughts" diamond. In this way, students are able to provide their own strategies about preventing the spread of communicable diseases.

As an extension of this assignment, students may continue their research to determine the effectiveness or viability of their recommendations. Students proceed down the Diamond Thinking handout until they've completed their assignment. It is easy to see how Diamond Thinking can act as a springboard for a variety of extension activities.

Diamond Thinking Handout

By Robert E. Berkowitz

While you're researching your topic, use the graphic organizer below to record and think about what you've read, heard, or viewed. This exercise will help you become a divergent thinker and will help you expand your ideas as you gather (engage and extract) information from sources.

1. In the "Information" diamond below, list facts you've read, heard, or viewed about your topic.
2. In the "My Thoughts" diamond, list your thoughts, feelings, experiences, or unanswered questions that relate to your facts in the "Information" diamond.

Topic:_____

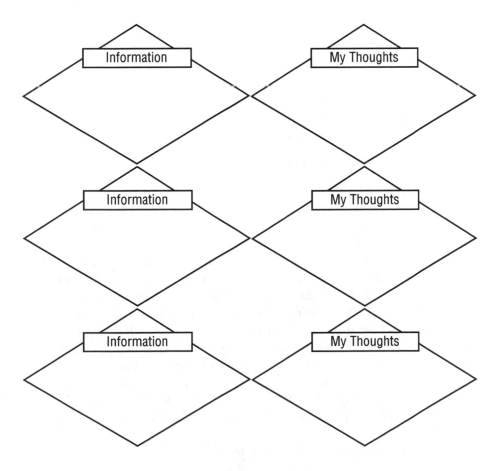

Title: *Insights Through Web Sites*

Author: Robert E. Berkowitz

Related Big6 Skills: Big6 #4—Use of Information

Purpose: This lesson will help students learn to evaluate Web sites carefully and critically.

Learning Contexts: Grades 6-12

Discussion: As we all know, the Internet can be a wonderful research tool. We also know that the information found on the Internet is generally unedited and that its nature is dynamic; it is there one day and gone the next.

When students access information on the World Wide Web we want them to be able to decide if the information is useful, reliable, and appropriate for their assignment.

One way to achieve this instructional goal is to teach students to "test" the Web site and information by using a set of criteria. Asking a series of general questions provides a strategy that is transferable to a full range of web-based and other information sources. Some sample questions follow:

- Who is the author or which institution sponsors this Web page?
- Who is the audience?
- What is the purpose of the information?
- How current is the information?
- Is the content accurate and objective?

Item: Web Site Analysis worksheet

Sample in Context: John DonVito, a social studies teacher at Wayne Central Schools (Ontario Center, NY), and I developed an activity that would focus on social studies content and essential World Wide Web skills. The activity, "Insights Through Web Sites," was prepared for a course titled "Participation in Government" and focuses on information found on Presidential candidates' Web sites. Students were asked to complete a Web Site Analysis Worksheet that was designed to review and refocus students' attention on the key questions to consider when assessing information found on Web sites. These considerations had been introduced and taught previously in other integrated units. The Insights through Web Sites worksheet features a series of generic Big6 Skill # 2—Information Seeking Strategies, Big6 Skill #3—Location & Access, and Big6 Skill # 4—Use of Information questions. A simple idea? YES. An idea that teaches transferable skills? YES. An instructional idea that can act as a springboard for your own creativity? ABSOLUTELY!

Insights Through Web Sites: Evaluating Information

Site name:

Site address:

Author:

Date Visited:

> **Directions:** There are no editorial review boards responsible for information published on the Internet. It is essential that you learn to review Web sites critically. Below are some questions that will help you evaluate Web sites and the information found on them.
>
> Look at the Web site carefully and answer the following questions with a yes or no and then add your own comments.

Design	
Does the site appeal to you visually?	
Does the site use design features that maximize the Internet's potential with features like sound and video?	
Do the graphics enhance the site's content?	
Do both the internal and external links work properly?	
Is the material structured coherently?	
Navigation	
Is it easy to understand how to move around the Web site?	
Do you have clear choices about how to find more information?	
Can you go back and forth within the page without getting lost?	
Does the site have an internal search engine?	

Authority (Author)	
Is it easy to determine who the author or authors of the Web site are?	
Are sources cited?	
Is there a link so that you can contact the authors with questions or feedback?	
Content/Accuracy	
Does the page title reflect its content?	
Do the authors clearly state their objectives? If so, do you believe that the authors met their objectives?	
Is the information well organized?	
Is the material updated frequently and is the last date of update visible?	
Is the information unbiased and balanced?	
If the authors have a particular point of view or agenda, are they forthright about their bias?	
Did the site enhance your knowledge of the subject?	
Does the site provide information that is not readily available from other sources?	

Insights Through Web Sites. Copyright © 2000. Big6 Associates, Inc.

Comparing the Presidential Candidates' Views

Directions:

Each political candidate has a position on the issues listed on this chart. Be prepared to present your findings to the class in a discussion that compares the candidates' positions on the issues.

Gun Laws	
Environment	
Abortion	
Trade	
Taxes	
Social Security	
Medicare	
Foreign Policy	
Education	
Defense	
Affirmative Action	

Title: *Three Across*

Author: Robert E. Berkowitz

Related Big6 Skills: Big6 #4—Information Use

Purpose: This generic note-taking strategy helps students focus information in a linear way.

Learning Contexts: Grades 6-12. This note-taking organizer is useful for middle school and high school students who benefit from a structured studying approach.

To use this tool, students begin by listing the important questions that need to be answered, then students find and note the answers from their content reading, viewing, or listening. Finally, students can jot down any supporting details or evidence that might help to explain or clarify answers to key questions.

This graphic organizer is especially useful while students are reading, listening, or viewing information. Students learn to engage information in an active way. They ask key questions to help guide their reading and look for specific answers to help focus their attention.

The Three Across method may be transferred from this worksheet to simply drawing lines on a blank sheet of notebook paper, and labeling the three columns. Then 1-2-3 work begins!

Discussion: Using this linear organizer, students can practice Use of Information note-taking skills in many situations and in a full range of content areas.

Students may use the Three Across organizer to take notes while reading a textbook assignment, or to gather and prepare information for an oral presentation. When students read a textbook, they need to look for general answers to the question and specific details for support. Writing assignments may also be structured by using this organizer.

Students may incorporate graphics such as editorial cartoons, charts, graphs, and other visual information. This simple, structured format provides students with a prepared set of notes they can use to complete homework assignments or to study for tests.

Item: Three Across handout

Sample in Context: Miss Maxon wanted to ensure that students would pay attention to a videotape on the Holocaust. Even though there was high interest in the video, she wanted to make sure that they didn't miss the details. As part of her lesson development, Miss Maxon pre-viewed the video and listed the first key question, the answer, and two details across the top of her Three Across sheet. This created a worksheet model for students. Before showing the video to her class, Miss Maxon explained the Three Across method. Next she played the first few minutes of the video where the question and answer were discussed. Miss Maxon once again pointed out where in the videotape she got the key question, the answer, and the details for her worksheet model.

After answering students' questions about the strategy, she continued to show the video in predetermined segments to help students better engage the content, and to help them focus on active viewing and listening.

By the end of the video, students had a set of useful notes that could be used for class-room discussion. Miss Maxon had evidence that students had really listened to a video that was important to the curriculum. The students were actively engaged, and she had evidence.

Three Across Handout

By Robert E. Berkowitz

#1—Questions	#2—Answers	#3—Important Details

This note-taking strategy will help you focus information in a linear way. You may use this sheet to prepare for an essay test, to organize facts from a reading assignment, or to gather facts for a writing assignment.

#1—Questions: List the important questions that need to be answered.

#2—Answers: Find and list the answers.

#3—Important Details: List any specific supporting details.

Reflections

CHAPTER 10

Big6™ #5: Synthesis

T his Chapter focuses on the Big6 #5–**Synthesis**—bringing all the information elements together to show what you've learned. In the Synthesis stage, researchers will do the following:

5.1 Organize information from multiple sources.
5.2 Present the result.

Big6 TIPS: Synthesis—Putting it All Together

Synthesis is the result, the output part of the information process. It's also the most visible part of the process. And, Synthesis takes place in every information problem-solving situation. Yes, Synthesis includes writing a research paper or report or creating some form of project. But, Synthesis is also:

- Answering multiple choice, fill-in, or short answer questions on a test
- Writing an essay, short story, or poem
- Creating a poster, overhead transparency, audiotape, TV show, multimedia presentation, or Web page
- Making a decision (e.g., what college to attend, which product to buy, whether to invest in a stock or mutual fund, where to go for dinner), or
- Communicating in person, writing, telephone, via e-mail, chat, or videoconferencing.

All these are forms of Synthesis for individuals or small groups. On the societal level we have Synthesis through communications and mass media—television, radio, books, magazines, newspapers, videos, CD music, computer games and simulations, and, of course, the Internet and WWW. Synthesis is certainly a big part of our society. When people speak about the information explosion, they are talking about being overwhelmed by the amount and forms of Synthesis.

As noted, from a Big6 perspective, Synthesis includes two aspects—organizing information and then presenting it. According to Wurman (1989) in *Information Anxiety*, there are a number of ways to organize information:

- By category (and subcategory)
- As a continuum (small to large or low to high, or the reverse)
- Alphabetically
- By time
- As a story (from beginning to end)
- Or as any combination of the above.

One interesting organizing (Big6 #5.1) activity to do with people of all ages is to bring in a collection of some kind (e.g., a music CD collection) and have groups decide how they would organize it. Also, ask them about various collections that they have—videos, toys, books, and dolls—and how they organize them. See if you can tease out the various options noted above for organizing information without having to present them yourself.

My favorite Big6 #5.1 exercise is to break a class into groups of five and give each group a manila envelope with 15 pictures in it. The pictures were cut from old magazines and are placed in no particular order, but I don't tell the groups that, of course. The task for each group is to organize the pictures in some way so they "make sense to them," to give the set of pictures a title, and to explain to the rest of the class how they organized the pictures. This leads to an entertaining session that usually results in some groups organizing by categories (e.g., people, places, and things), others develop a storyline around the pictures (e.g., a day in the life of…), and various other combinations of approaches. I always give as little direction as possible. In particular, I will only answer a key question if asked: "Do we have to use all the pictures?" My answer is rhetorical: "When we gather information for a project or report, do we have to use all the information that we find?" Clearly not.

Teaching forms of presenting, Big6 #5.2, is as important as working on organizing information. For example, consider the types of synthesis products that most students complete—homework, handouts, tests and quizzes, papers, and projects. One Big6 tip is to have students consider alternatives from a checklist when faced with presenting— alternatives in terms of time and effort as well as effectiveness in relation to the task. There's an important link between Synthesis and Task Definition, and I often suggest discussing "what the result should look like" as part of Task Definition and remembering, "what was the original purpose" as part of Synthesis.

Technology also plays a big role in Synthesis. Think about all the computer software intended to help people present ideas and information: word processing, desktop publishing, graphic programs, audio/video editing, *PowerPoint* and presentation software, electronic spreadsheets, and even databases. Synthesis is a major industry in the world because you can have the best ideas, solutions, or insights in the world, but if you can't express them you are nowhere.

Therefore, it makes sense to integrate teaching software for Synthesis in the context of the Big6 process and real curriculum or personal needs. Students are highly motivated, and it is easy to demonstrate how they can save time and effort—and do a better job—by using technology in meaningful, contextual ways.

Title: *I-Search*

Author: Kathleen L. Spitzer

Related Big6 Skills: All

Purpose: Students will research a topic and record their progress in a journal.

Learning Contexts: Appropriate for middle school students.

Discussion: Instead of doing research, students can do an I-Search. The I-Search paper requires students to monitor the processes they use rather than the outcome or product (ex. a report or project). The focus is on learning how to learn.

Through the I-Search process, students are guided to think of a topic and identify pertinent background knowledge they have about the topic. They are prompted to think of questions, then to seek answers for them. Throughout the I-Search, students record their progress in a journal using Big6 terminology. The teacher or library media specialist can react to the journal entries on a periodic basis. Students will evaluate themselves as researchers at the conclusion of the project.

Item: I-Search Journal

Students are instructed that they will be doing an I-Search rather than a research paper. They should be told that they will examine a topic of interest and will be required to record their activities in a journal. The teacher or library media specialist should use a sample I-Search to provide students with an example. Students should be reminded that at the conclusion of the I-Search, they will write an evaluation of their skills.

Sample in Context: Mrs. Gionet didn't look forward to the 8th grade research paper she assigned during the second semester each year. After talking with the library media specialist, Mrs. Gionet decided to assign an I-Search project instead of a research paper. At first, students found the concept difficult. They wanted to do a report, turn it in, and be done with it. The I-Search process required them to think about their research techniques and the Big6 Skills they were using. When the I-Search project was complete, students remarked that they found it valuable and would like to do it again.

I-Search
Sample Worksheet

Name: ____*Mrs. Spitzer*____ Period: _____

Describe your topic here: ____*Rap Music*____

In five minutes, write everything you already know about your topic.

Z89 seems to play a lot of rap music. I don't usually like rap — in fact, when my kids change the car radio station to Z89, I ask them to change it back. I've heard of Ice T and Kris Kross. It seems that some rap is violent. Ice T was in the news this past summer for one of his songs.

Think about your topic. Use this page to write some questions that you hope to answer through research.

What is the history of rap?

Is all rap violent?

Who are some current rappers?

What do students at our school think of rap?

Review what you already know about your topic. Read through the questions you hope to answer. Use this space to describe the focus of your I-Search.

I think I will investigate the history of rap. Where and when did it start? I would also like to know what people think of rap.

Keywords!

Rap, rapper

Information Seeking Strategies

Use the list below to prioritize possible information sources for your I-Search.

___General Information Sources (Encyclopedias, etc.)

___Books—Use the online catalog to search

___Magazines—Use MAS or Reader's Guide

___People—Arrange an interview. Write out questions first!

___Resources File—Use the contents folder in the reserve room

___Reference Books—See the library media specialist for suggestions.

I-Search Journal

Use the space below to record your notes in the Information Use process. Include the date when making journal entries.

Sample journal entry:

11/15/99 – Since my topic is historical, I decided to use the online catalog. I used a keyword search and typed in the word "Lincoln."

11/2/99 – I decided to start looking for information by using MAS. I typed in rap and the computer found lots of articles. I looked at and selected some articles from our library.

Got Newsweek magazine and started reading about rap. Found out that all rap is not violent. Some kids like rap and think it will eventually bring racial harmony.

11/3/99 – Used the online catalog and searched by using the keyword "rap". Found that we have two books. One of them, The Mouse Rap, is non-fiction. (It looks interesting – I think I'll read it. Maybe I can use it for this report.) I got the book Hip Hop the Illustrated History of Break Dancing, Rap Music and Graffiti. Started reading and found the history of rap. Realized that hip hop is another term that I could use for a keyword. I think I'll try that in MAS tomorrow to see if I get any more citations.

Evaluation!

Use the space below to describe what you learned about the process of doing your I-Search.

Example: My topic was Kris Kross. I learned that because I was trying to find current information, I should have used MAS instead of the online catalog.

I learned that I can get more information about a topic by using a variety of keywords.

I learned that I need to allow myself more time to take notes because I am a slow writer!

I don't think I'll try to do a model next time. I'm not very good at putting models together. A poster might be a good substitute. I am good at drawing.

Title: *"I-Search"* **PowerPoint** *Presentation*

Author: Robert Darrow

Related Big6 Skills: Big6 #5—Synthesis, #6—Evaluation

Purpose: This lesson will help students learn to create a Microsoft *PowerPoint* presentation on an "I-Search" topic.

Learning Contexts: Grades 6–12

Discussion: Students typically complete an "I-Search" paper at some point in their school career. Why not create it as a *PowerPoint* presentation and have students present this in front of the class? This type of process also would work well for a "senior showcase" project where students present their best work in front of a panel of judges (parents or teachers). Blending text and pictures is a crucial Synthesis skill in business as well as education. People remember information much better when they have to put pictures with words and then present the information to a group.

Microsoft *PowerPoint* is the suggested program to use because *PowerPoint* is typically used by people in the business world. Many companies have hired high school students to create *PowerPoint* presentations for various business projects.

Item: *PowerPoint* Evaluation

Note: This project works best when there is at least one computer for every two students.

This project can be completed in one week whether students have worked in *PowerPoint* before or not. Students should plan some type of layout or make notes about their topic on paper before beginning this project.

PowerPoint presentation tutorials will guide students through basic *PowerPoint* vocabulary such as *slide view, slide show view, slide sorter view*, etc. Choose a layout in *PowerPoint* that has a title, picture, and text on each slide. For this project, students create nine slides. In most cases, nine slides will fit on one 3.5" disk. Instruct students to create the slide layout for all nine slides before adding text.

Guide students to create slides in this order and to label slides as follows:
1. Title of Topic and Authors
2. Why I Chose this Topic
3. What I Already Know and Where I Got This Information
4. Main Point 1
5. Main Point 2
6. Main Point 3
7. Conclusion
8. What I Learned
9. Bibliography / Source List

Next, have students add all of their text. As a general rule, there should not be more than three main points on each slide, and no slide should have more than 25 words. Experts say that people can not remember more than 25 words or three main points per slide. Microsoft teaches presenters the "6 by 6 Rule." Each slide should have no more than six lines with no more than six words on each line. The words should be in phrases and not in sentences. Once all text is placed, then students can add pictures and other special effects. It is important that students complete the text prior to adding pictures. Students need to learn that the content of the words is what demonstrates their knowledge of a topic and is the most important part of a good *PowerPoint* presentation.

Evaluation: Teachers can view the *PowerPoint* projects on each computer as they are finished or each student, or group of students, can formally present their project in class while the teacher scores the project. Some options for student driven evaluation might include: having students complete evaluation sheets on several projects, having groups of students all viewing different presentations at the same time and completing a peer evaluation form, or having students complete a self-evaluation form on their project and then turning the project in on disk. See the *PowerPoint* Evaluation worksheet for one example of a student evaluation form.

To receive an "A," students must **Save** the project on a **disk** and:

- Include everything in the "*PowerPoint* layout"
- Have a picture on each slide
- Include all text, with no more than three main points or 25 words per slide
- Use easy to read text
- Use easy to read colors, text, and pictures.

Sample in Context: Students in virtually every school subject can create *PowerPoint* presentations. Students are motivated to prepare an appealing presentation when the audience is their peers or adults. *PowerPoint* presentations can be effective for learning about theorems in geometry, a step-by-step guide in constructing a model in a drafting class, synthesizing important concepts in foreign language, demonstrating the causes of a war, or identifying the important elements of a novel. Scanned pictures or digital photos can be used in presentations. Electronic portfolios can be created using *PowerPoint*. *PowerPoint* provides an excellent way to bridge student learning from the world-of-school to the-world-of-work.

PowerPoint Evaluation

Scoring Guide: 3 - Outstanding; 2 - Good; 1 - Needs Improvement

Presenter:_____

Circle score for each item.

A.	Content is clear..	3	2	1
B.	Easy to read..	3	2	1
C.	Layout of slides makes it easy to understand the content............................	3	2	1
D.	Nicely blended text and pictures...................	3	2	1
E.	No more than 20 words per slide..................	3	2	1
F.	Pictures nicely arranged.	3	2	1
G.	Background enhances presentation.................	3	2	1
H.	Use of animation......................................	3	2	1
I.	Good transitions.......................................	3	2	1
J.	Overall oral presentation...........................	3	2	1
K.	Overall Score..	3	2	1

Comments:

One thing I liked about this *PowerPoint* presentation is....

One way to improve this presentation would be....

Created by Robert Darrow, July, 1998

Title: *Planet* HyperStudio *Project*

Author: Robert Darrow

Related Big6 Skills: Big6#5—Synthesis

Purpose: The purpose of this lesson is to help students synthesize their knowledge about various aspects of the nine planets.

Learning Contexts: *HyperStudio* allows students to Synthesize information from a variety of sources and put it into a presentation that can be shown to one other person or to an entire class. The use of *HyperStudio* as an authoring software allows students to demonstrate and show their knowledge for most any concept.

Discussion: Using computer software programs is an excellent motivator for students to learn any material. Part of the beauty of the Big6 is that it can be applied to any project, whether print or digital. It is not as effective to have a Synthesis activity without first knowing the Task Definition or Evaluation component. Students need to know what is required for the Synthesis step before they can be successful in completing any school assignment. Therefore, it is important that the Task Definition and Evaluation steps be considered prior to beginning the Synthesis step. In this example, there are two Synthesis activities: creating a *HyperStudio* presentation and then presenting the information to classmates.

Sample in Context: The seventh grade science teacher wanted students to have a better understanding of the nine planets. The students gathered all of the necessary components and information in the classroom before coming to the library media center to complete the Synthesis activity in *HyperStudio*. Specific aspects of planets that he wanted students to address included: order of planets, composition, atmosphere (what kind of life can live there?), length of revolution and rotation (length of day and year or time it takes to circle the sun), distance from sun, number of moons and the number of probes that have been sent there from Earth.

Students decided how to use *HyperStudio* to present the information. As partners, students had to create one card for each planet, which included the content aspects as outlined by the teacher. They made Synthesis decisions in the design of each card including the background color, text color, positioning of pictures and buttons, illustrations, sound effects, and animation.

Once the *HyperStudio* stacks were completed, then students presented their information to the entire class. As partners, the students alternated between operating the computer presentation and reading the text they had written. Presentations were displayed on a big screen TV.

While students present anything to another person or to classmates, it is important to consider the Evaluation step of the Big6. Students naturally evaluate how they are doing during their own presentations. Observers naturally think to themselves, "this is cool!," "I wish I had done this to my presentation" or "they should have used lighter text with that dark background." The teacher not only looks at the presentation, but also should consider the content. This is where an evaluation assessment scoring guide can be useful. The guide may be used by classmates for peer evaluation or may be used just by the teacher for evaluation purposes.

Title: *Putting it Together*

Author: Kathleen L. Spitzer

Related Big6 Skills: Big 6 #5—Synthesis

Purpose: Use this lesson to demonstrate how information can be organized.

Learning Contexts: Apply this lesson across subject areas in secondary and higher education settings where students need to organize information.

Discussion: Many students are able to gather information but have difficulty organizing information. By using the "putting it together" transparencies (or slides) followed by a couple of organizational techniques, the teacher or library media specialist will demonstrate how information can be organized by category.

First, the teacher or library media specialist will make a brief presentation about organizing information. Then the teacher or library media specialist can demonstrate how such a project could be organized. The teacher can brainstorm a topic and show the different types of notes that might have been gathered. Next the teacher can write these topics on an overhead transparency or on the board to create a mind map. These topics can be connected to each other to create categories. Categories can then be indicated by color.

Students can analyze the information they have gathered and determine how the information will fit into the categories. They can create a mind map indicating the categories that they have brainstormed. Students can use various colored highlighters to create a color-coding scheme to indicate these categories on their notes. When it is time to synthesize, students gather together all the notes of a particular color and arrange them in a logical order.

Item: Mind Map handouts

Sample in Context: A high school music class was assigned to do a report on a popular musician or on a musical instrument. After students gathered their information, the library media specialist used the "Putting it Together" overheads to demonstrate how information could be organized. He created a mind map for a music project (see figures 1 and 2).

Students analyzed their own information and determined appropriate categories. The teacher helped any students who had difficulty selecting categories. Students then used colored highlighters to indicate these categories on their notes. Students who took notes on cards found this particularly useful since they could then separate their cards by color and further organize their information. Other students had used the photocopy and highlight method of taking notes. These students used their colored highlighters to indicate the categories at the top of the photocopied article. They then sorted their photocopies by color and began to organize their information.

Figure 1

Mind Map

Mozart

Beethoven

Rock

Bluegrass

Heavy Metal

Jazz

Classic Rock

Elvis

Rap

The Beatles

The Rolling Stones

Classical

Country

Bach

Figure 2

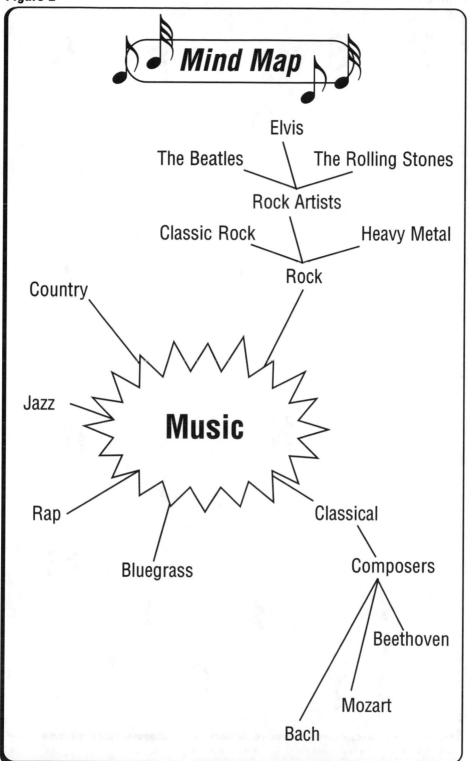

Figure 3

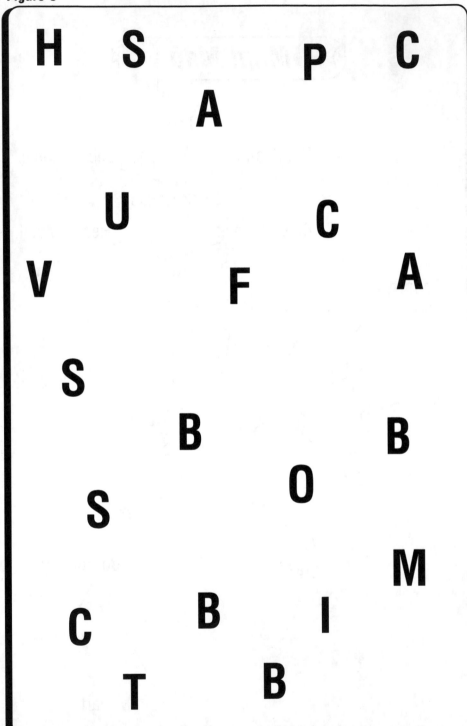

Note: Use figures 3-5 for more practice in organizing and grouping information

Figure 4

UFO

HBO

PBS

CIA

ABC

CBS

MTV

Figure 5

MTV

HBO

UFO

PBS

CIA

ABC

CBS

Title: *Puzzle It*

Author: Kathleen L. Spitzer

Related Big6 Skills: Big6 #5—Synthesis

Purpose: The purpose of this lesson is to demonstrate how information can be organized.

Learning Contexts: Apply this lesson across subject areas in secondary and higher education settings where students need to organize information.

Discussion: Once students have gathered their research for a task, they face the daunting chore of putting it all together. This is not an easy task for anyone. It takes perseverance and selectivity. An experienced writer knows that gaps might be identified while putting together the final project and more information might be needed. Also there may be some information that was found during the research phase that is interesting but that just doesn't fit into the final product.

Using simple geometric shapes, students can experience a simulation of putting together various types of information. Most students will find that they needed just one more shape of a certain type or that they had some shapes left over that they didn't want to use. This process parallels the writing process.

Item: Putting the Pieces Together

Objective: Students will experience a Synthesis activity and create conclusions about how information is put together to form a unified product.

Materials:

- Numerous geometric shapes (small, medium, and large squares, rectangles, and equilateral triangles) cut out of poster board. (Tip: It helps if the equilateral triangles have been cut so that the sides are the same size as the sides of the squares.) Fluorescent poster board is eye-catching.
- 16 medium size clasp envelopes
- Putting the Pieces Together overhead master (see attached).

Preparation:

Divide the shapes into 16 envelopes so that each envelope has a good mixture of all the different shapes.

Directions:

- When the class is seated at tables (you can group desks together if necessary), distribute one envelope for each pair of students.
- Tell students that they will do an activity with the shapes in the envelope.
- Tell students they will have a limited amount of time to cooperate with their partner to make anything they want out of the shapes.
- Tell students that they may not trade shapes with other pairs of students. They must use only the shapes that came in their envelope.

- Ask students to begin. Walk around the room to monitor activity.

- After the specified amount of time, tell students to stop.

- Ask students to get up and walk around the room to view the other creations.

- Ask students to take their seats again.

- Ask students for their reactions to the activity. See if students mention that they did not have enough shapes. If no one says this, you can ask a question. You can also point out that you noticed that some people had shapes leftover. Ask if anyone felt that they ran out of time. Ask students to think about the writing process ahead of them. Ask if they can draw some parallels with the activity that they just completed. Show the "putting the pieces together" overhead to demonstrate how pieces should form a unified whole.

- Ask students to put the shapes back in the envelopes.

Sample in Context: Students in French class were assigned to write a one-person play about a famous French person and to perform that play for the class. After working with the students to find information from a variety of sources, the teacher had students use the Puzzle It activity to demonstrate that as they put together their research, they might find that they needed more information. They might also need to leave out some interesting information that they found along the way in order to create a more consistent project.

Putting the pieces together . . .

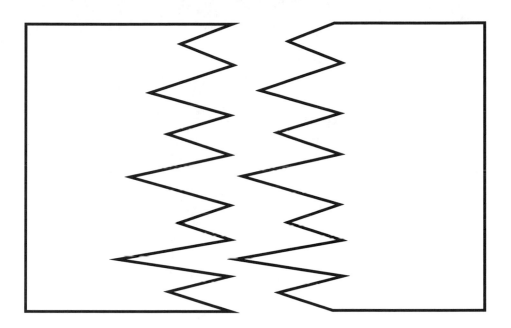

. . . to form a unified product.

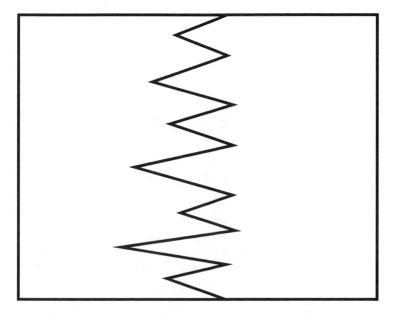

Reflections

CHAPTER 11

Big6™ #6: Evaluation

T he last stage of the Big6 is #6–**Evaluation.**

    6.1 Judge the result (effectiveness).
    6.2 Judge the process (efficiency).

Big6 TIPS: Evaluation—Ensuring Effectiveness and Efficiency

Assessing effectiveness and efficiency of the process is crucial to success in infor-mation problem-solving. However, students often leave this step out—in part, because they are rarely taught to engage in self-assessment. Evaluation is a crucial component of the Big6 process. Students should be able to do the following:

■ Engage in concrete tasks of reflecting and responding to predetermined criteria

■ Determine the strengths and weaknesses of their solutions

■ Justify their decisions based on criteria

■ Understand the value of using a process to solve information problems, and

■ Become self-directed and self-motivated to produce quality work.

When students evaluate themselves, they assume control and responsibility for their own work and become active participants in their learning. The role of the teacher becomes a guide, coach, and facilitator rather than the center of all knowledge and ultimate arbitrator.

Feelings are also important in evaluation. Students may lack confidence and pride in their work because they don't really know whether or not they have done a good job. Or, feelings of confidence and pride are replaced with frustration and disappointment when they get their assignment back with a poor grade when they expected to do well. From a Big6 perspective, we want students to apply the same evaluation criteria as teachers do to student work. Students need to learn to look at their work through their teachers' eyes. In this way, students can build on strengths and identify areas for improvement. Students gain insight into specific areas to improve their performance. This can boost confidence, pride, and result in a higher level of academic success.

Students of all ages can engage in evaluation activities. For example, with pre-K and kindergarten students, we teach "before you are about to turn in your work, stop a minute and think, 'Is this okay? Is this what I want it to be? Did I do what I was supposed to? Should I work a little more, make a change, do something else—or is it good enough?'"

The same review should be done with older students. Teach them to evaluate their process when they think they are ready to turn in a project. This reflection is a key part of students' improving as information problem solvers.

Effectiveness–6.1

Evaluating effectiveness means looking at the result, or culmination of the information problem-solving process. This result might be a paper, report, project, or even a test. Evaluating effectiveness means judging how well one did in meeting the goals of the information problem-solving process.

In effectiveness, students learn to judge their products. Students can learn to diagnose the result of their effort when they learn to do such things as the following:

- Compare the requirements to the results
- Check the appropriateness and accuracy of the information they use
- Judge how well their solution is organized
- Rate the quality of their final product or performance compared to their potential (i.e., Did I do the best that I could?), and
- Judge the quality of their product to a predefined standard.

Students can learn how to judge their own effectiveness. Some techniques to facilitate learning effectiveness include:

- Have students assess themselves before turning in their assignment. This will give them a basis to compare what they think versus what the teacher thinks.

- Use rubrics or scoring guides. Show students how you use these and then have students create scoring guides themselves.

- Have groups of students assess sample work that you provide—bad examples are often the best way to get students to recognize quality.

It is useful to help students think about effectiveness. This can be a tricky concept, but students of all ages can learn it. I like to start by using examples of effectiveness in other settings, such as sports and business. In sports, effectiveness means winning (and, of course, feeling okay about yourself). In business, effectiveness means making a profit (and also making a contribution to society). Discussing how to be effective in these situations gets students thinking about how they can be equally effective in school.

Efficiency–6.2

The other part of evaluating an information problem-solving process is thinking about efficiency. Efficiency means saving time and effort in the process. This is certainly something to which most students can relate.

Remind students that the goal in school is to do as well as possible with as little time and effort as possible. They may be surprised to hear that saving time and effort in schoolwork is okay as long as it results in a quality process. How can students be efficient and still be successful? The answer is, by honing their Big6 Skills.

Determining efficiency is as complex as dealing with effectiveness. Improving efficiency involves evaluating the nature, tendencies, and preferences of their personal information problem-solving process. This is sometimes referred to as "meta-cognition" —recognizing how we learn, process information, and solve problems. From a Big6 perspective, we can help students learn how to assess the efficiency of the process they use to reach decisions and solutions. Some techniques to facilitate learning and to evaluate efficiency include encouraging students to do the following:

- Keep a Big6 log of information problem-solving activities; periodically evaluate how you are doing

- Reflect back on the sequence of events and judge effort and time involved

- Review and analyze the areas of frustration and barriers they came up against, and

- Rate their abilities to perform specific information problem-solving activities (i.e., locating, note-taking, skimming, scanning, and prioritizing).

Here's a general tip for improving both 6.1 and 6.2. For important assignments, I like to have students include a one-page assessment summary of their processes and the assignment. I want to know what worked and what didn't. If they could do it over, what would they do differently? If they could change one thing, what would it be? Then give credit for being insightful—after all, recognizing what one needs to do and to learn is most of the battle.

Title: *Creating Women in History Web Pages*

Author: Robert Darrow

Related Big6 Skills: Big6 #5—Synthesis, Big6 #6—Evaluation

Purpose: The purpose of this lesson is to create a Web page about a selected woman in history.

Learning Contexts: Grades 6-8

Discussion: Students need the opportunity to create Web pages in the context of learning. They can learn to organize and present their ideas on the Web the same way they organize and present their ideas in a traditional written report. Almost any curriculum project can be presented as a Web page. To accomplish this as a class project, it is helpful to have at least one computer for every two students. Most word processing programs today have "Web making" or "html" features built into the software. Consider creating a Web project after students have had some experience on the World Wide Web. This project may be completed by individuals, partners, or small groups.

Creating Web pages motivates most students. In addition to learning the topic, students learn important points of Web page creation such as colors to use, font sizes to use, and how to design the page. Various successful Web page topics include: ancient Japanese culture, personal heritage, animal classifications, and authors.

Item: Woman in History Web Page Requirements, Women in History Web Page Layout, Web Page Evaluation

In class, students learned about women in history. The classroom teacher wanted the students to gain a deeper understanding of different women in history. Students came to the library media center with the name of a woman in history, notes about the woman, and an outline of what content was needed for their Web page.

Your Web page must include the following:

1. Title: Who are you researching? When did she live?
2. Your first name, school, and grade level.
3. Purpose of this Web page.
4. Where was your woman born? Where did she live?
5. What were her achievements, and when did she accomplish them?
6. What did your woman contribute to history? For what is she famous?
7. Why is this woman so wonderful? Why did you choose this woman?
8. Show at least two different pictures of your woman in history.
9. Bibliography—Provide a list of Web sites and print sources you used to gather this information.

Evaluation:

An "A" would include:

- All information listed above
- At least two pictures pertaining to your woman
- Text that is easy to read (no more than 25 words per section)
- Colors and pictures that blend nicely.

Page 170 shows one example of a Web page evaluation. The World Wide Web also provides many Web evaluation guides. The Global Schoolhouse (*http://www.gsn.org*) has the most extensive Web evaluation guide for students. Their evaluation guide is part of their yearly "Thinkquest" student Web making project.

Sample in Context: When students know that their work will be seen by more people than just the classroom teacher, they prepare projects differently. Web pages allow students to have a world audience for their work, or at least a school-wide audience. Students enjoy showing finished projects that have been done at school to parents who have World Wide Web access. Knowing that other people will see their work is strong motivation to produce quality Web pages.

In addition to student Web pages about women in history, students produced Web pages about Japanese culture, favorite authors, personal heritage, and careers. Linking the students' Web pages together and posting the pages on the school or district Web server is the time consuming part of this project.

Women in History
Web Page Requirements

NOTE: This can be used as a handout for students or as a Web page.

You will be creating a "woman in history" Web page which includes information about you, your family, and your ancestors. To start the Web page, open Microsoft *Word*. Go to File/New. Click on "Web Page" tab. Choose "blank Web page." See the sample layout below.

Your Web page must include the following (See sample below):

1. Title: Who are you researching? When was she alive?
2. Your first name, school, and grade level.
3. Purpose of this Web page.
4. Where was your woman born? Where did she live?
5. What were her achievements and when did she accomplish them?
6. What did your person contribute to history? For what is she famous?
7. Why is this woman so wonderful? Why did you choose this woman?
8. Show at least two different pictures of your woman in history.
9. Bibliography – Create a list of Websites and print sources you used to gather this information.

Evaluation

An "A" would include:

- All information listed above
- At least two pictures pertaining to your person
- Easy-to-read text (no more than 25 words per section)
- Nicely blended colors and pictures.

Woman in History
Web Page Layout

Woman's Name
by Your First Name, Name of School, Grade

Purpose: This Web page was created as an assignment in my history class. This Web page discusses (woman's name), who is an important woman in U.S. History.

Background—Who is she? Where was she born and raised? Where did she live?	What did your person contribute to history?
What were your woman's major accomplishments?	Why was this person so wonderful? Why did you choose her?

Bonus: Create a timeline of your woman's life. Include at least eight items.

Websites I used:

Date Completed:

Web Page Evaluation

Scoring Guide: 3 - Outstanding; 2 - Good; 1 - Needs Improvement

Web Page Title/Subject:_____

Item	3	2	1
A. Purpose is clear			
B. Easy to read			
C. Layout of page(s) makes it easy to understand the content			
D. Nicely blended text and pictures			
E. Text content makes sense			
F. Pictures load easily and are nicely arranged			
G. Background enhances Web page			
H. Links work			
I. Date and information in bottom left hand corner			
J. Overall rating			

Comments:

One thing I liked about this Web page is....

One way to improve this Web page would be....

Created by Robert Darrow, April, 1998

Title: *Individualized Information Problem-Solving Profile*

Author: Kathleen L. Spitzer

Related Big6 Skills: Big 6 #6—Evaluation

Purpose: In this assignment, students create a profile of their interest, confidence, apprehension, and satisfaction as they proceed through an information problem.

Learning Contexts: This lesson is applicable across subject areas in secondary and higher education settings where students have an extended assignment.

Discussion: Kuhlthau (1985) demonstrated that while people solve an information problem they may progress through a variety of emotions. We have all heard our students moan as they receive an extended assignment. They are expressing their emotions at that point and this is consistent with Kuhlthau's research. Students may be apprehensive about the assignment and wonder about their ability to complete it.

The Big6 provides students with a framework for accomplishing their task in an organized fashion. By using the Individualized Information Problem-Solving Profile, students can keep a record of their emotions as they proceed through a task. Upon completion of the task, students can analyze their charts and see how their emotions changed as they completed each step of the information problem solving process.

An awareness of emotions can provide students with a greater level of confidence the next time they approach an extended task. Students will be cognizant of their emotions and of their ability to work through a task to its completion.

Item: Individualized Information Problem-Solving Profile

Sample in Context: The Participation in Government policy issue assignment is particularly difficult. Students are required to research a policy issue and:

- Give the background and history of the issue
- Examine both sides of the issue
- Design and carry out a survey regarding the issue
- Provide a solution to the issue supported by evidence of why that particular solution would work.

The assignment is a group project, and students have a number of weeks to complete and synthesize their research. The group presents their policy issue to the class for 45 minutes. Each group member must participate in the presentation, which must include graphs relating to the survey and an audio-visual component.

Students are especially daunted by this assignment. Students are apprehensive just thinking about all of the work involved and the 45-minute presentation to the class.

Students tracked their emotions as they worked through the project by using the Individualized Information Problem-Solving Profile. While reviewing their charts, students had an opportunity to analyze their emotional responses to completing such a task.

Bibliography:

Kuhlthau, C. C. (1985, Winter). A process approach to library skills instruction. *School Library Media Quarterly*, 14, 35–40.

Name: _____

Date:_____

Individualized Information Problem-Solving Profile

Directions: The Individualized Information Problem-Solving Profile is designed to help you record the emotions you may experience as you solve an information problem. It is important that you follow the directions on each page.

The Big6™ Skills

Task Definition:	Defining the problem and identifying the information requirements of the problem.
Information Seeking Strategies:	Determining the range of possible sources. Evaluating and prioritizing the range of possible sources
Location & Access:	Locating sources and finding information within the sources.
Information Use:	Reading, hearing, or viewing the information in a source. Extracting the information from a source.
Synthesis:	Organizing information from multiple sources. Presenting information.
Evaluation:	Determining the effectiveness of the product and the efficiency of the information problem-solving process.

Source:
Eisenberg, M.B., & Berkowitz, R.E. (1988). *Curriculum initiative: An agenda and strategy for library media programs.* Norwood, NY: Ablex Publishing Corp.

Interest

Directions: At points indicated throughout the information problem-solving process, place a mark on the scale below to indicate your feelings at that particular time.

Beginning
Immediately after you have received the problem:

Uninterested · Interested

Task Definition
After defining the task:

Uninterested · Interested

Information Seeking Strategies
After determining and prioritizing possible information sources:

Uninterested · Interested

Location & Access
After locating sources and finding information:

Uninterested · Interested

Information Use
After using the information:

Uninterested · Interested

Synthesis
After organizing and presenting the information:

Uninterested · Interested

Evaluation
After evaluating the product and the process:

Uninterested · Interested

Acknowledgement is given to Michael B. Eisenberg for the presentation format of the charts on this page.
Copyright © Kathleen L. Spitzer, 1990.

Confidence

Directions: At points indicated throughout the information problem-solving process, place a mark on the scale below to indicate your feelings at that particular time.

Beginning
Immediately after you have received the problem:

Uninterested   Interested

Task Definition
After defining the task:

Uninterested   Interested

Information Seeking Strategies
After determining and prioritizing possible information sources:

Uninterested   Interested

Location & Access
After locating sources and finding information:

Uninterested   Interested

Information Use
After using the information:

Uninterested   Interested

Synthesis
After organizing and presenting the information:

Uninterested   Interested

Evaluation
After evaluating the product and the process:

Uninterested   Interested

Acknowledgement is given to Michael B. Eisenberg for the presentation format of the charts on this page.
Copyright © Kathleen L. Spitzer, 1990.

Apprehension

Directions: At points indicated throughout the information problem-solving process, place a mark on the scale below to indicate your feelings at that particular time.

Beginning

Immediately after you have received the problem:

Worried   Not worried

Task Definition

After defining the task:

Worried   Not worried

Information Seeking Strategies

After determining and prioritizing possible information sources:

Worried   Not worried

Location & Access

After locating sources and finding information:

Worried   Not worried

Information Use

After using the information:

Worried   Not worried

Synthesis

After organizing and presenting the information:

Worried   Not worried

Evaluation

After evaluating the product and the process:

Worried   Not worried

Acknowledgement is given to Michael B. Eisenberg for the presentation format of the charts on this page.
Copyright © Kathleen L. Spitzer, 1990.

Satisfaction

Directions: At points indicated throughout the information problem-solving process, place a mark on the scale below to indicate your feelings at that particular time.

Beginning
Immediately after you have received the problem:

```
|___|___|___|___|___|___|___|___|___|___|
```
Dissatisfied   Satisfied

Task Definition
After defining the task:

```
|___|___|___|___|___|___|___|___|___|___|
```
Dissatisfied   Satisfied

Information Seeking Strategies
After determining and prioritizing possible information sources:

```
|___|___|___|___|___|___|___|___|___|___|
```
Dissatisfied   Satisfied

Location & Access
After locating sources and finding information:

```
|___|___|___|___|___|___|___|___|___|___|
```
Dissatisfied   Satisfied

Information Use
After using the information:

```
|___|___|___|___|___|___|___|___|___|___|
```
Dissatisfied   Satisfied

Synthesis
After organizing and presenting the information:

```
|___|___|___|___|___|___|___|___|___|___|
```
Dissatisfied   Satisfied

Evaluation
After evaluating the product and the process:

```
|___|___|___|___|___|___|___|___|___|___|
```
Dissatisfied   Satisfied

Acknowledgement is given to Michael B. Eisenberg for the presentation format of the charts on this page.

Directions: Use this form to record one-word descriptions of your emotions other than those on the last four pages.

Problem-Solving Process	Emotion
Immediately after receiving the problem:	
After defining the task:	
After determining and prioritizing possible information sources:	
After locating sources and finding information:	
After using information:	
After organizing and presenting information:	
After evaluating the product and the process:	

Acknowledgement is given to Michael B. Eisenberg for the presentation format of the charts on this page.
Copyright © Kathleen L. Spitzer, 1990.

Title: *Monitor Your Emotions*

Author: Kathleen L. Spitzer

Related Big6 Skills: Big 6 #6—Evaluation

Purpose: The purpose of this assignment is to allow students to create a profile of their interest and confidence as they proceed through an information problem.

Learning Contexts: This lesson is applicable across subject areas in secondary and higher education settings where students have been given an extended assignment.

Discussion: This worksheet is a much abbreviated version of the Individualized Information Problem-Solving Profile. This worksheet asks students to monitor their confidence and interest in the task. However, the worksheet could be adapted to represent any emotion that the teacher wants the students to track.

It can sometimes be difficult for students to persevere as they complete an assignment. Some students lack self-confidence and may want to give up before they have even started. The Monitor Your Emotions worksheet will help students become aware of the pattern of their emotions as they proceed through assignments. If students realize that they frequently feel a low level of confidence as they begin a task but that this level will increase as they complete the task, they may be able to recognize this the next time they approach an extended task. They will be cognizant of their emotions and of their ability to work through a task to its completion.

Item: Monitor Your Emotions handout

Sample in Context: The Environmental Science class members are required to choose an environmental problem, investigate it, and make a one-hour presentation to the class. Students in this class have a wide range in their abilities to tackle such an assignment.

To ease students' discomfort, the library media specialist pointed out to the class that people progress through various emotional states as they solve an information problem. Students then tracked their own levels of confidence and interest as they completed the project.

Monitor Your Emotions

Directions: Use the chart below to monitor your emotions throughout your project. Place a dot on the chart indicating your confidence and interest levels at particular dates.

5= High   **1=Low**

Confidence

5											
4											
3											
2											
1											

Date

Confidence

5											
4											
3											
2											
1											

Date

Directions: In the spaces provided below, note your reactions to the project.

_____

Date:

_____

Date:

_____

Date:

_____

Date:

_____

Date:

_____

Date:

_____

Date:

Title: *Rate Your Partner*

Author: Kathleen L. Spitzer

Related Big6 Skills: Big 6 #6—Evaluation

Purpose: The purpose of this assignment is to allow students to comment on how effectively their partner(s) worked with them on a project.

Learning Contexts: This lesson is applicable in any subject areas in secondary and higher education settings when students need to complete an assignment with a partner or partners.

Discussion: We often require students to work together but don't give them an opportunity to comment on the effectiveness of their partners. Furthermore, we don't often provide the partners with feedback relating to their contributions to the entire project.

Since group projects and cooperative learning are becoming a focus of many educational and corporate environments, an awareness of our contributions as partners is important.

The Rate Your Partner form provides students with a way to comment on their partners' contributions. Partners can then review the form and note how they might improve their contributions in the future.

Item: Rate Your Partner handout

Sample in Context: Students in the Spanish I class had to select a city in Spain and create a tri-fold travel brochure for the city. The purpose of the brochure was to create an interesting leaflet that would make people want to visit that city. Students worked in pairs and the final assignment was to include the following:

- Pictures of at least three tourist attractions in the city
- Descriptions of the three tourist attractions
- A map of the location of the city in relation to the rest of Spain
- The exchange rate for pesos.

Many students worked very well together. Other students had difficulties because a partner was constantly absent or refused to contribute his or her fair share of the work effort.

The Rate Your Partner form gave students an opportunity to comment on their partner's performance and to review their own contributions.

Name:_____ Date:_____

Partner's name: _____ Period: _____

(*Rate Your Partner*)

Rate your partner using the scale below: (Circle one choice for each category.)

Participation: How much did your partner participate?
1. Did not participate at all
2. Did not participate much
3. Participated
4. Participated actively

Cooperation: How cooperative was your partner?
1. Not cooperative at all
2. Somewhat cooperative
3. Cooperative
4. Very cooperative

Contribution: How much did your partner contribute?
1. Did not contribute anything
2. Contributed a little
3. Made contributions
4. Made substantial contributions

Comments: Use this section to make specific comments on how well your partner worked with you to complete this project.

Total score: _____

Title: *Self-Reflection Checklist*
Evaluation Checklist: Research Paper

Authors: Sandra Baker and Kathleen L. Spitzer, Library Media Specialists, Cicero-North Syracuse High School, Syracuse, New York; Jean M. Davis, Maine

Related Big6 Skills: Big 6 #6—Evaluation

Purpose: This lesson provides students with assessment tools that will help them reflect on the effectiveness of their product and the efficiency of their information problem-solving process.

Learning Contexts: This lesson is applicable across subject areas in secondary and higher education settings where students have been given an extended assignment.

Discussion:

Student (speaking to library media specialist): "I need one more source for my paper about abortion."

Library media specialist: "What type of information about abortion do you need?"

Student: "I dunno. I just need one more source."

Library media specialist: "Do you need statistics about abortion?"

Student: "I don't care. I just need one more source."

As this conversation demonstrates, some students tend to focus on turning in an end product regardless of the quality of that end product. They just want to "get it done." They become consumed by finishing the task and don't take the time to evaluate their end product prior to submitting it to the teacher. A checklist can help focus students' attention on the effectiveness of their product and the efficiency of their information problem-solving process. Students should use these checklists prior to turning in their assignment and make any necessary changes to their end product.

Item: Self-Reflection Checklist

Sample in Context: Students in an 11th grade English class had to write a paper relating the works of an author to a theme. The assignment asked them to:

- Choose an author with whom they were familiar
- Create a thesis statement relating the author's works to a theme
- Analyze at least three (3) of the author's works by referring to literary criticism
- Use at least ten (10) sources (including the primary works being analyzed)
- Write a paper that is at least six (6) pages long using in-text citations and including a works cited page in the MLA format.

Using a checklist helped these students focus on the details of the assignment rather than on "just getting it done." The teacher remarked that the quality of papers seemed to be better than in past years when students had not used a self-reflection checklist.

Self-Reflection Checklist

How well did I complete the steps to success on this assignment?

1. I included all required information covering each portion of the assignment. A B C D F

2. I asked for help from the teacher or library media specialist when I had a question on the assignment. A B C D F

3. I developed a plan before starting to find information. A B C D F

4. I chose the best possible sources available to me. A B C D F

5. I asked for help from the teacher or library media specialist when I had difficulty finding information. A B C D F

6. I read, viewed, and listened carefully, making a conscious decision about what information to use and what information to discard. A B C D F

    a. I was able to read and use charts and graphs. A B C D F

    b. I was able to read and use maps. A B C D F

    c. I was able to understand and use illustrations. A B C D F

    d. I was able to read and use text. A B C D F

7. I organized my information using a plan or outline. A B C D F

8. I created a final product consistent with the assignment. A B C D F

9. I reviewed and revised my product before producing a final copy. A B C D F

10. I attempted to find and change problem areas. A B C D F

Some of the strengths in completing this assignment were:

_____

_____

_____

_____

Some of the changes I would make next time I complete an assignment are:

_____

_____

_____

_____

Evaluation Checklist: Research Paper

Before you turn in the final copy of your paper, use this checklist to determine how it measures up. After your evaluation, make any necessary changes.

1. The topic of the paper is focused and reflects the assignment.
   a. Yes
   b. No

2. The purpose is clear and is to:
   a. inform
   b persuade
   c. entertain
   d. combination

3. The title reflects the contents of the paper.
   a. Yes
   b. No

4. The first paragraph or section introduces the reader to the topic of the paper.
   a. Yes
   b No

5. Ideas are logically organized:
   a. around a time sequence
   b. by category
   c. from simple to complex
   d. in order of importance
   e. other planned presentation

6. Headings and sub-headings are used to indicate major and minor sections.
   a. Yes
   b. No

7. Ideas are supported (i.e. by using examples, statistics, anecdotes, quotations, etc.).
   a. Yes
   b. No

8. The ending summarizes the main points of the paper.
   a. Yes
   b. No

9. Writing is concise.
   a. Yes
   b. No

10. Words are used well and the same words are not repeated too often.
    a. Yes
    b. No

11. Paper is free of errors in grammar, punctuation, and spelling.
    a. Yes
    b. No

12. Sources are properly cited in a bibliography.
    a. Yes
    b. No

13. Bibliographic references conform to a common style and format.
    a. Yes
    b. No

14. Paper is typed or word processed and neat.
    a. Yes
    b. No

Adapted by Kathleen L. Spitzer from: "Evaluating Your Article—A Check Sheet for Writers." In Jerry Apps, *Tips for Article Writers*, Wisconsin Regional Writers Association, Madison, WI, 1973. pp. 14-15.

Title: *Students as Self-Assessors*

Author: Jean M. Davis

Related Big6 Skill: Big6 #6—Evaluation

Purpose: These personal assessment questions help students analyze progress throughout a writing assignment.

Learning Contexts: This lesson is applicable across subject areas in secondary and higher education settings where students have been given an extended assignment.

Sample in Context: Jean Davis, an educator in Maine, developed these personal assessment questions that help the student analyze progress throughout a writing assignment.

After the first week:

1. What have you done to begin your search since the project was introduced a few days ago?
2. What will be your next step?
3. What aspect of the search will prove the biggest challenge for you? Why? What will you do to try to handle this challenge?

After the second week:

1. List the items of progress which you have accomplished on your search since the first day the project was introduced.
2. What is your next step and how will you go about it?
3. Tell of one exciting, discouraging, or satisfying experience you've had since undertaking your search.
4. Are you having problems with your search? If so, what are they?

After the third week:

1. What have you accomplished so far in your search?
2. Number and list the items of significant progress (e.g. purchasing a two-pocket folder for your drafts is not significant progress!)
3. Which experience since you've started your search has helped you make major progress? Why?
4. Identify at least one of your strengths which is helping you succeed.
5. What would you do differently another time? Why?

Davis, J. M. (September, 1991). Students as Self-Assessors, in *News & Views in English Language Arts*, a publication of the Maine Council for English Language Arts, (15)1.

Reflections

Reflections

CHAPTER 12

Closing
The Pervasive Big6™

O ur work with the Big6 has resulted in our seeing the world through "Big6 glasses." In other words, it seems that we are constantly coming across events and actions that relate to the Big6 in every area of life. This shouldn't come as a great surprise, because there is growing recognition of the extent to which information literacy and information skills pervade everyday life.

This fact was made clear in an episode of the television show *The Simpsons*. In this episode, Bart must learn to play miniature golf to prepare for a competition. He is at a complete loss about how to approach the problem and turns to his sister, Lisa, for help. A trip to the library gives them the information they need to make Bart a successful miniature golfer. In solving this information problem, the Simpson children use all stages of the Big6:

- **Task Definition—focusing on the problem and the information requirements**
- **Information Seeking Strategies—using the library**
- **Location & Access—using the library catalog**
- **Use of Information—reading and sharing information**
- **Synthesis—applying "geometry" to the golf problem**
- **Evaluation—realizing that it worked.**

Another example of the widespread applicability of the Big6 is in the movie *Apollo 13*. In one part of the film, a broken air filter threatens to cause the spacecraft to run out of breathable air. To save the astronauts' lives, the ground crew must make a different type of air filter work in place of the broken one by using only the materials the astronauts have available. After a good deal of experimentation, the ground crew solves the information problem just in time. As with the *Simpsons* example, the people in the *Apollo 13* film can be seen using all of the Big6 steps with special emphasis on Task Definition, Information Seeking Strategies, Use of Information, and Synthesis. Solving this information problem is one of the most exciting points in the movie.

Use of the Big6 can also be seen in sporting events. A football game, for instance, is essentially an information problem—pitting one information system against another. To win, the coaches need to gather, assess, and synthesize information from the situation (such as weak areas of the other team and strengths of his/her own team) and use this information to devise a winning strategy (for example, which play to run). Ultimate evaluation is very easy to determine—check the scoreboard at the end of the game.

The idea that "information is everywhere" is the basis of our view of information literacy. Information is a pervasive and essential part of our society, and indeed, our lives. We are, at our essence, processors and users of information. This is not a recent development. Humans have always been dependent upon information to help make decisions and guide our actions. Change has come in the sheer volume of information and the complexity of information systems—largely due to advances in information technology.

Recognizing the pervasive nature of information and the importance of information problem-solving skills is the key to where we, as educators, are and where we are going. It is our responsibility to understand the nature of information and the way that people use it. We can ensure that all individuals have the opportunity to learn the information literacy skills they will need in the future to successfully navigate the future landscape of information.

Summary

Information problem-solving is a basic component in effective instructional programs. The Big6 Approach to Information Problem-Solving:

Level 1: Information Problem-Solving
Whenever students are faced with an information problem (or with making a decision that is based on information), they can use a systematic, problem-solving process.

Level 2: The Big6 Skills
1. Task Definition
2. Information Seeking Strategies

3. Location & Access
4. Use of Information
5. Synthesis
6. Evaluation

Level 3: Components of the Big6 Skills

1. Task Definition
    1.1 Define the problem
    1.2 Identify the information requirements of the problem
2. Information Seeking Strategies
    2.1 Determine the range of possible sources
    2.2 Evaluate the different possible sources to determine priorities
3. Location & Access
    3.1 Locate sources
    3.2 Find information within sources
4. Use of Information
    4.1 Engage (e.g., read, hear, view) the information in a source
    4.2 Extract information from a source
5. Synthesis
    5.1 Organize information from multiple sources
    5.2 Present information
6. Evaluation
    6.1 Judge the product
    6.2 Judge the information problem-solving process.

The benefits of the Big6 Skills' broad-based approach to information problem-solving include the following:

- Improved instructional practices
- Provision for individualization and adaptability of the process to all students' learning styles
- Clear definition of the requirements of good units and lessons from an information perspective
- Provision of a framework for the analysis of existing instructional units and lessons
- Provision of a structure for results-based assessments.

Reflections

Appendix

Appendix A: Comparison Chart

Eisenberg/Berkowitz Information Seeking (The Big6 Skills)	Kuhlthau Information Problem-Solving	Irving Information Skills	Stripling/Pitts Research Process	New South Wales Information Process
1. Task Definition 1.1 Define the problem 1.2 Identify info requirements	1. Initiation 2. Selection 3. Formulation (of focus)	1. Formulation/analysis of information need	1. Choose a broad topic 2. Get an overview of the topic 3. Narrow the topic 4. Develop thesis/purpose statement	Defining
2. Information Seeking Strategies 2.1 Determine range sources 2.2 Prioritize sources	4. Exploration (investig. info on the general topic)	2. Identification/appraisal of likely sources	5. Formulate questions to guide research 6. Plan for research & production	Locating
3. Location & Access 3.1 Locate sources 3.2 Find info	5. Collection (gather info on the focused topic)	3. Tracing/locating individual resources		
4. Information Use 4.1 Engage (read, view, etc.) 4.2 Extract info		4. Examining, selecting, & rejecting indiv. resources	7. Find, analyze, evaluate resources	Selecting
		5. Interrogating/using individual resources 6. Recording/storing info	8. Evaluate evidence take notes/compile bib.	Organizing
5. Synthesis 5.1 Organize 5.2 Present	6. Presentation	7. Interpretation, analysis, synthesis and eval. of info. 8. Shape, presentation, and communication of info	9. Formulate questions to guide research 10. Create and present final product	Presenting
6. Evaluation 6.1 Judge the product 6.2 Judge the process	7. Assessment (of outcome/process)	9. Evaluation of the assignment	(Reflection point—is the paper/project satisfactor)	Assessing

References

Akin, L. (1998). Information fatigue syndrome: Malady or marketing? *Texas Library Journal, 74*(4).

American Association of School Librarians and Association of Educational Communications and Technology. (1998). *Information power: Building partnerships for learning.* Chicago: American Library Association.

Ball, L. (1952). I love Lucy: The classics [Video]. Available from Amazon.com, http://www.amazon.com.

Barry, C. L. (1994, April). User-defined relevance criteria: An exploratory study. *Journal of the American Society for Information Science, 45*(3), 149-59.

Drucker P. (1992, December 1). Be data literate—know what to know. *Wall Street Journal*, p. A16.

Eisenberg, M. B., & Berkowitz, R. E. (1996). *Helping with homework: A parent's guide to information problem-solving.* Syracuse, NY: ERIC Clearinghouse on Information & Technology.

Glanz, W. (2000, February 28). Information overload weighs down web. *Insight on the News, (16)*8, 27.

Gross, M. (1998). Imposed queries in the school library media center: A descriptive study. *Dissertation Abstracts International, 59*(09), 3261. (University Microfilms No. 9905536).

Guernsey, L. (2000, June 29). The search engine as cyborg. *New York Times*, p. D1.

Information Fatigue Syndrome. (1996). *Investor's Business Daily.*

Koberg, D., & Bagnall, J. (1980). *The universal traveler: A soft-systems guide to creativity, problem-solving and the process of reaching goals.* William Kaufman, Inc.

Kuhlthau, C. C. (1985). *Teaching the library research process.* West Nyack, NY: The Center for Applied Research in Education.

Kuhlthau, C. C. (1993). Implementing a process approach to information skills: A study identifying indicators of success in library media programs. *School Library Media Quarterly, 22*(1), 11-18.

Lewis, D. (1996). *Introduction to dying for information.* [Online]. Available: http://about.reuters.com/rbb/research/dfiforframe.htm.

Noller, Parnes, & Biondi. (1976). Creative problem solving model. In *Creative behavior workbook.* New York: Scribner.

Pappas, M., & Tepe, A. (1997). *Pathways to knowledge: Follett's information skills model kit.* McHenry, IL: Follett Software.

Shenk, D. (1997). *Data Smog.* New York: Harper and Collins. In Kerka, S. (1997). Information Management. *ERIC Digest.* [Online]. Available: http://www.ericacve.org/docs/mr00009.htm

Stripling, B. K., & Pitts, J. M. (1988). *Brainstorms and blueprints: Teaching library research as a thinking process.* Englewood, CO: Libraries Unlimited.

Wurman, R. S. (1989). *Information anxiety.* New York: Doubleday.

[1] AskERIC—http://www.askeric.org
[2] Internet Public Library—http://www.ipl.org/
[3] Netscape—http://www.netscape.com/
[4] Yahoo—http://www.yahoo.com/
[5] AltaVista—http://www.altavista.com
[6] Lycos—http://www.lycos.com/
[7] Hotbot—http://hotbot.lycos.com/
[8] AskA+ Locator—http://www.vrd.org/locator/index.html

Index